A Garland Series

Accounting History and the

A thirty-eight-volume facsimile series

Development of a Profession

Edited by *Richard P. Brief*, NEW YORK UNIVERSITY

The General Principles of the Science of Accounts

and

The Accountancy of Investment

Charles E. Sprague

GARLAND PUBLISHING, INC.
NEW YORK & LONDON
1984

For a complete list of the titles in this series
see the final pages of this volume.

Library of Congress Cataloging in Publication Data

Sprague, Charles E. (Charles Ezra), 1842–1912.
The general principles of the science of accounts ;
and, The accountancy of investment.

(Accounting history and the development of a profession)
Reprint (1st work). Originally published in 12
installments in a magazine published by the School of
Commerce, Finance & Accounts at New York University in 1901.
Reprint (2nd work). Originally published: New York :
Business Pub. Co., 1904.
1. Accounting—Addresses, essays, lectures.
2. Investments—Accounting—Addresses, essays, lectures.
I. Sprague, Charles E. (Charles Ezra), 1842–1912.
Accountancy of investment. 1984. II. Title: General
principles of the science of accounts. III. Title:
Accountancy of investment. IV. Series.
HF5625.S755 1984   657   84-10247
ISBN 0-8240-6336-8 (alk. paper)

The volumes in this series are printed on
acid-free, 250-year-life paper.

Printed in the United States of America

Editor's Note

This book reprints two lecture series by Charles Ezra Sprague who pioneered the development of accounting theory in the United States. The first of the lecture series, "The General Principles of the Science of Accounts," appeared in twelve installments in 1901 in a magazine published by the School of Commerce, Accounts and Finance at New York University. The contents of these lectures are related to Sprague's earlier articles, "The Algebra of Accounts" (1880), and to his more well-known and now classic text, *The Philosophy of Accounts* (1907). None of the standard works on the literature of the period make reference to "The General Principles" and one might suppose that accounting historians and others interested in the development of accounting thought simply are not aware of these important lectures. This volume now makes them available.

The other book reprinted in this volume is *The Accountancy of Investment*, originally published in 1904. It went into several editions and, after Sprague's death in March, 1912, was included in a revised and expanded text by Leroy L. Perrine in 1914. The text included this and other work by Sprague on the mathematical aspects of accounting, mainly issues related to interest and present value, including the problem of accounting for bonds. Nearly 70 years later Paton wrote in the foreword to the 1972 Scholars Book Co. reissue of *The Philosophy of Accounts* that *The Accountancy of Investment* was "an outstanding work" and "superior on all counts to anything in this area that has been published since."

Contents

The General Principles of
the Science of Accounts

THE GENERAL PRINCIPLES OF THE SCIENCE OF ACCOUNTS.*

A Course of Lectures delivered before the School of Commerce,
Accounts and Finance, New York University, 1900-1901,
by Col. Charles E. Sprague, A. M., Ph.D., C. P. A.,
President of the Union Dime Savings Institution.

Revised for Commerce, Accounts and Finance.

I.

The Science of Accounts, which is now for the first time to be treated as a branch of university study, has in the past received but little attention, and has been confused with the art of bookkeeping. But while bookkeeping is a beautiful and a difficult art, it is only one of the five or six arts which depend upon the principles of the Science of Accounts. The bookkeeper is the practitioner of one of these arts; but there are others.

THE KINDRED ARTS.

We may reckon as such arts the following:—
The keeping of accounts, the verification of accounts, the interpretation of accounts, the utilization of accounts, the creation of systems of accounts.

BOOKKEEPING.

We have, first, bookkeeping, the keeping of accounts. The difference between the person who keeps accounts skilfully and the skilled accountant who understands his science is like the difference between the skilful engineer who can run a complicated engine —run it well and make it perform all its functions, and the mechanician who is able to build that engine, or repair it, or take it to pieces, or, when necessary, invent another one for special purposes.

AUDITING.

The verification of accounts is a second art. This is the art of the auditor—the power of criticising the work of the bookkeeper. This branch presupposes the power to keep books and much besides.

ACCOUNTANCY.

We have a third branch of the profession, which is the interpretation of accounts; and this is accountancy proper. It is the function of the accountant to take the dry details of facts and figures, and transform them into something that shows a meaning: he makes a history instead of a diary. The diary will give facts from day to day, but an historian will marshal these facts into a comprehensive narration that tells the growth, progress and tendencies of a nation. So the accountant can take the dry figures which merely show details of purchase and sale and contracts and indebtedness, etc., and make out from them a history of a certain business or enterprise or financial department, and show to those interested at the end of the period what has been done, and wherein it has succeeded and wherein it has failed.

SYSTEM-BUILDING.

Then there is the creator of systems; and this, as we rise higher in the sphere, becomes confined to fewer persons, and is still more important and of higher utility—the power to construct systems of accounts for special purposes, for any purpose that may be required, from the humblest commercial enterprise to the accounts of the United States Treasury.

It was supposed in the earlier days, before accountancy became established as a profession, that books

could be kept only in one way, and that way was almost precisely the same as that described in the work of an Italian author, dated 1494, the earliest book on the subject in existence. He was more pious than the bookkeepers of later days, as he has begun his inventory, "In the name of God, amen." His method of actually keeping the books did not differ very much from the method of fifty years ago, and which is still in vogue to a great extent. There was the same plan of keeping the three books—the day book, the journal, and the ledger. The day-book was necessary, as our author says, in which to write down the transactions as they occur, merely describing the how, the when, the where, from whom, and to whom; and "this may be done by thy servant or by thy wife in the absence of the skilled scrivener," who can afterwards put these details into order in a book which is called the journal. So his day-book was simply a rough memorandum, and it was necessary then because the scrivener was an unusual man. He made his periodical visits for the purpose of writing up the books. His Sundries debtor to Sundries, etc., By Capital to Cash, and other mystic terms were very impressive to the good merchants of Venice. This man was thought to be a man of rectitude, and to possess many secrets unknown to the rest of the world. This plain method of sorting out transactions into the ledger through the medium of the journal was, I think, the only method known in this country fifty or sixty years ago. There has been a wonderful gain made since then by doing the same thing by wholesale, and at the same time making a saving of three-fourths of the ledger formerly used. The devising of these systems, and applying them to special businesses, is systematology, and is another branch of the accountant's art.

BUSINESS MANAGEMENT.

But last of all, we come to what has been touched upon in some things said before—the utilization of accounts, the making use of the records of the figures which are kept in order by the bookkeeper, which are verified by the auditor according to systems provided by the accountant and interpreted afterwards by the accountant in a form the most succinct, to be utilized by the administrator or the business manager. The business manager in modern days is a great power, the one who shapes the workings of the vast concerns that are now occupying the commercial field. The manager of a business has to be somewhat of an autocrat. He must know, just as a general knows from the reports of his subordinates, what is going on all over the field. He himself cannot attend to all the details of the business, and he must draw his information from the records kept by the bookkeeper and verified by the auditor and carried out on lines devised and supervised by the accountant. And this last is one that may seem to you who are not engaged in active business or do not expect to be, and to those of you who expect to take up the professions, as belonging to the duty of the bookkeeper. So it is no wonder that the science of accounts has been looked upon as something less than it really is when it has been confused with the mere art of bookkeeping. It is quite another matter, and not to be by any means included in the same category.

NAME OF THE SCIENCE.

We have not any one word to express this science that we are trying to reduce to a code of principles.

Almost all other sciences have a single word by which they can be referred to, but we have to say "the science of accounts." However, there have been several attempts to devise a better name. The true name would be *logistics*, but this has been pre-empted: it is used in military science, and may be explained as being the art of assembling and moving troops and supplies. I suppose we shall have to let the military authorities retain the word. There was an older Greek word that might have been used, but it refers specifically to what we now call the cash account. We are cut off from Latin in the same way, as the appropriate term, ratio, has been used in connection with metaphysics and mathematics. A suggestion has been made that we adopt the French original of the word account, "compte," and make a compound of it, namely, Comptology. Some bolder genius has suggested the word Accountics, and I rather think that that has a chance of sticking.

NOT AN ACCOUNT, BUT ACCOUNTS.

We say the science of accounts. That is very expressive. We do not say the science of an account. If you know all about how to handle a single account, that would be only a small portion of the task. There is a method, an inferior method, depending for its principles on this science, but using them very limitedly, called single-entry bookkeeping. In this, one account has no real and necessary connection with another; they are kept separately. This can hardly be called the art of accountancy. In the science of accounts, it is not merely a question of keeping correctly separate, detached accounts, but it is an aggregation of accounts, accounts considered as a whole, depending upon each other as do the members of the planetary system. Accounts of detached matters do not come under the head of the science of accounts; they are simply the A-B-C. We have got to deal with a system of accounts before we can say we are handling the science.

WHAT IS AN ACCOUNT?

When we say account, we do not mean simply the ledger account; the word has a very extended meaning. As the account is the basis of all our dealing, we want to get at a definition of that, at least enough of a definition for the present purpose. I am not much of a believer in definitions. I think that by the time a man has got to where he can give a perfect definition, he does not need the definition. Now, the word account has a number of meanings, from where we say cash account, merchandise account, to the phrase, "Postponed on account of the weather." The broadest definition I can give of an account is that it is a *statement of facts;* but that is too broad. Not every statement of facts is an account. A rambling tale told by a gossip would not be called an account, because it is not systematic. An account is *a systematic statement of facts.* If we go a little closer, we see that a more specific meaning is, that it tends to some purpose. An account has a bearing on something. We say, "How do you *account* for this?" We mean that the person to whom this is addressed shall pile up evidence of some sort which will lead to a conclusion. Therefore we shall narrow the definition. By account, then, we mean *a systematic statement of facts leading to a conclusion.* Now, is that all? Besides facts leading to a conclusion, there must, in the nature of things, be some of them favorable to that conclusion and some of them adverse, at least, it is apt to be so. There

is seldom an account of anything which goes entirely by positives—where all the evidence is on one side. The other side will undoubtedly have something to show. Therefore, I should, in bringing it down to a scientific and technical definition, say that it is *a systematic record of facts of a similar or opposite tendency leading to a conclusion.*

But we must limit our definition still more to make it fit the accounts of which this science treats, that is, accounts of value, or accounts of finance. And thus we arrive at our complete definition:—

AN ACCOUNT IS A SYSTEMATIC RECORD OF FINANCIAL FACTS OF A SIMILAR OR OPPOSITE TENDENCY, LEADING TO A CONCLUSION.

AN ACCOUNTING.

In a large number of instances the conclusion that is sought to be reached by an account is for the relieving of some person of responsibility. We see in this the genesis of almost all the accounting in ancient times which our Dean laid before us. Therefore I have used a word which we have in English which makes a very nice distinction—an *account* and an *accounting.* Every accounting is an account, but not every account is an accounting, that is to say, not all accounts are constructed for the purpose of relieving somebody of responsibility or justifying some resolution. Some accounts, the majority of accounts, that are now kept in modern business, are simply for the purpose of giving information, so that we will speak of an *account* in general, and we will speak of an *accounting* when we mean such an account as leads to a conclusion relieving some person of responsibility or supporting some resolution. That, I think, is as definitely as we need to analyze the account at this stage. We have got to see it more closely at hand to understand what it is, and then we must go on and find its relation to other things. I think this definition will do fairly well for a beginning, and we will adopt that, unless at the next meeting, when we open the floor for debate, some of you gentlemen have objections to it.

PURPOSE OF ACCOUNTS.

The next point you will want to know is, What are the objects of keeping accounts? Why did we want to have any accounts? Well, these objects, I think, are twofold; and each of the branches which I shall mention will be twofold, also. The first object is information; the second object is protection.

INFORMATION.

In seeking information there are always two opposite tendencies or requirements, or rather, there is a requirement for minute information, and a requirement for comprehensive information; and that has been a difficulty in probably every system of bookkeeping or every system of accounts that ever existed—the struggle on the one hand to give the minutest details required, and the desire on the other hand to group the information so as to give a comprehensive result. One we need for one purpose, one we need for another. For instance, a mercantile firm wishes to know the cost and the profit, and the number of the salesmen, and the price that the goods brought, and whether it was in cash or in credit, and upon what dating it was sold, and to whom it was sold, etc., etc. And yet all these details alone would never give them at the end of the year such information as would enable them to tell what the history of the business had been. There has to be more comprehensive information somewhere. And all systems of bookkeeping endeavor to reach these two extremes as far as needful or necessary—to give in some accessible way when needed the most minute information, and, on the other hand, to give the broadest and most comprehensive information. In business of any magnitude, it pays to have not exactly two systems, but to have the extremes in the same system that will give both of these particulars to the greatest extent possible. A compromise is generally disastrous to both, for it is usually not minute enough for some purposes, and not sufficiently comprehensive for others.

PROTECTION.

Now, I said that we need accounts for information and for protection. There are two kinds of protection needed—outside protection and inside protection. If a man did not delegate any of his powers, as was the case with people in ancient times, he need never fear anything from the inside; he does not delegate anything, and he cannot be defrauded. All he needs is correct accounts from the outside world. But the instant he begins to delegate, he has got to trust somebody, and while he can never make it impossible, he can make it very difficult for that somebody to defraud him—by systems of accounts, which in various ways make the process difficult, and, second, make the detection of the fraud possible. Probably no system will insure the instantaneous detection of fraud; but methods have been devised, and are constantly in use, which give information that will with certainty lead to ultimate discovery, and make it very difficult for the defaulter to cover up his tracks. As to outside protection, we need that class of accounts which are called personal, which enable us to establish our rights against other people, and enable us to fulfill our obligations towards other people; so that our rights and obligations are both justly and equitably met and enforced—so that our obligations are not made excessive by someone else's claim, which we cannot dispute because of our lack of evidence, and that our own rights shall be preserved, and our claims against others shall be fully met and no diminution of our claims permitted.

*

THE GENERAL PRINCIPLES OF THE SCIENCE OF ACCOUNTS.*

A Course of Lectures delivered before the School of Commerce, Accounts and Finance, New York University, 1900-1901, by Col. Charles E. Sprague, A. M., Ph.D., C. P. A., President of the Union Dime Savings Institution.

Revised for Commerce, Accounts and Finance.

II. FORM OF THE ACCOUNT.

Having established the definition of an account we must next decide what form it shall take. What arrangement is the best? Let us judge the question as if we were the first to whom it occurred.

First, we must segregate the figures representing the units of value from the context which explains them. No method of doing this can be more apposite than to place them in a vertical column. Besides the amount of the account, or transaction, it is necessary for us, at least in most cases, to show when the occurrence was; and it is proper in most cases to show why it was; and it is desirable in a vast number of cases to show with whom other than ourselves this occurred. Therefore, the account has the money column, as we call it, for figures; it has the date column, and usually the remainder of space is laid out without special subdivision. It is necessary to have the money column clear and free, for the purpose of examining the amount of the several items; it is necessary to have the date column clear and free, because we have to search that constantly for information; but it is not necessary to have the explanatory matter so divided off, because we do not ordinarily search through that for any one particular.

Fig. 1.

[Date]	[Specifications]	$
When	How Why With whom	How much

This is a frame into which may be fitted all amounts of the same kind or tendency; but the requirement for representing negatives or amounts of the opposite tendency at once introduces complication.

Now, the question is, where shall we put the several columns containing the When, the Why, the Whom, and the How Much of the negatives? The usual solution—the time-honored solution—which is probably the best for many purposes, is simply to duplicate the columns I have just mentioned, so that the items of the primary tendency shall have their date, consideration, personal, and value column; then they shall be followed by the corresponding columns for those of the opposite tendency, also arranged in the same order,

namely, the date, the consideration, the person, and the amount of value. That represents roughly the standard ledger account.

Fig. 2.
The Standard Ledger Account.

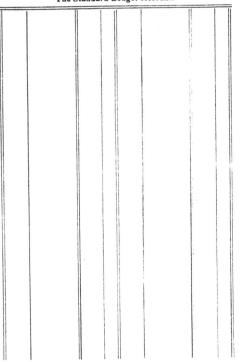

Here we have a double frame for the opposing facts. The great majority of ledgers, probably, throughout the entire world, have that precise arrangement. It was once considered a sin to deviate from it; but, if you can find any good reason for doing so, I think it is rather a merit.

For example, in some kinds of accounts it has been found very desirable that the values represented should be as close together as possible, where you want to compare the two items of opposite tendency. Hence, some people have placed both of the money columns directly in the center, and then reversed the order of the other columns, bringing the date to the extreme outside of each page.

Fig. 3.
Money Columns in the Centre.

Date		$		$		Date

Again, it has been found in some classes of accounts that one column required a great deal more space for explanation than the other. The secondary column, or negative column, being composed of things that were almost all of one tendency, required no explanation at all.

FIG. 4.
Unequal Division.

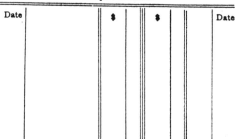

Still another variation. In all the arrangements so far considered the dates do not follow chronologically, but jump from side to side. If we desire to have the dates so arranged that they run consecutively, we may use but a single date column and a single specification column, but a pair of money columns.

FIG. 5.
Journal Form.

Date			$		$	

I mention these variations in form in order to suggest that substance is everything and conventional form is of minor importance.

THE ITEM.

We have now (1) defined the account; (2) given it a fixed form or frame. Next we must consider what is to be placed in the frame and how arranged.

As the account is the unit of the system, so the separate facts which compose it are its atoms. They are called items. The word has a curious history. It means in Latin, *also*, or *likewise*. It was customary to prefix it to each article in a bill of goods, after the first.

Each account, then, is composed of items. Let us take a few items and put them into the form of an account, selecting first, for reasons which will appear hereafter,

AN ACCOUNT OF PROPERTY.

The particular kind of property being immaterial,

we may select money as that kind which it will be the least trouble to value. Such an account is called a *cash account*, cash meaning, originally, a box.

The financial facts, of which a cash account constitutes a systematic record, are receipts and payments; the conclusion to which they lead is the amount of money on hand.

We must place the receipts on one side of the account form (Fig. 2) and the payments on the other side. At this stage, keeping but one account, it makes no difference which side; but as we expect to keep various accounts in correlation with each other, let us say, arbitrarily, that the left-hand side shall be for receipts and the right for payments.

Let the following be the items:—

(1) Jan. 1. Borrowed from A. B., $100.
(2) Jan. 31. Received salary, $50.
(3) Feb. 2. Repaid A. B., $75.
(4) Feb. 15. Loaned C. D., $35.
(5) Feb. 28. Received salary, $50.
(6) Mar. 1. Paid expenses, $49.
(7) Mar. 3. Repaid to A. B., $23.
(8) Mar. 5. Loaned to C. D., $12.
(9) Mar. 31. Received salary, $50.
(10) Apl. 10. Collected from C. D., $10.
(11) Apl. 15. Collected from C. D., $20.

These items, stated in the form of an account, will appear as follows:—

FIG. 6.
Cash Account.

Jan. 1	Borrowed from A.B.	$100	Feb. 2	Repaid A.B.	$75
" 31	Received Salary	50	" 15	Loaned C.D.	35
Feb. 28	Received Salary	50	Mar. 1	Paid Expenses	49
Mar. 31	Received Salary	50	" 3	Repaid A.B.	23
Apl. 10	Collected from C.D.	10	" 5	Loaned C.D.	12
" 15	" "	20			

Here are six items on the one side and five of opposite tendency on the other, and their nature may be represented by any pair of the following expressions:—

LEFT HAND	RIGHT HAND
Received	Paid
In	Out
Plus	Minus
Increase	Decrease
More	Less

The sum of the positive, or left-hand, items is $280; the sum of the negative, or right-hand, items is $194;

the resultant of these opposing forces is, therefore, $86, the amount on hand or conclusion sought. How shall this be represented?

The simple and most obvious way would seem to be as follows:—

FIG. 7.
Cash Account.

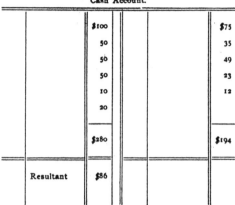

$100	$75
50	35
50	49
50	23
10	12
20	
$280	$194
Resultant $86	

But this is not the usual way.

BALANCING AN ACCOUNT.

If a pair of scales has different weights on the two sides, so as to be "out of balance," we usually add enough to the lighter side to produce equilibrium.

FIG. 8.
Large weight on left-hand scale marked P, smaller weight on right N, little weight to balance R.

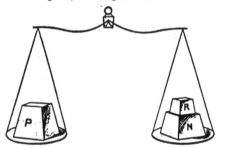

Similarly we add to the less side of the account enough dollars to make it balance, to put it in equilibrium. Thus:—

FIG. 9.
Cash Account.

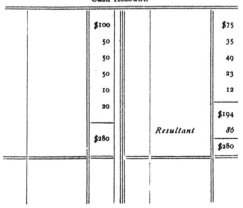

$100	$75
50	35
50	49
50	23
10	12
20	
	$194
	Resultant 86
$280	$280

I have inserted the "resultant" in italic to distinguish it from the items—to distinguish the conclusion from the facts leading to it.

Now the account expresses, asserts something. All arithmetical statements are made by means of an equation, and this account is thus made into an equation. It expresses the fact that the receipts are such and so much, aggregating $280; that the payments therefrom are such and so much, aggregating $194; and, as the conclusion, that the amount now on hand is $86. Or—

$$\text{Receipts} = \text{Payments} + On\ hand.$$
$$280 = 194 + 86.$$
$$\text{Ins} = \text{Outs} + Remainder.$$

In this last form the equation will apply to any property account. Increase of value (which may be from other causes besides acquirement) is recorded on the left-hand side of an account; the right-hand side contains two things quite at variance, one the decrease of property or of value, and secondly the *resultant*, or value in possession. This resultant is not an occurrence, but a conclusion.

Such is the accountant's way of expressing his conclusions—by an equation, not by a subtraction. The whole theory of accounting systems depends upon this.

AN ACCOUNT OF INDEBTEDNESS.

To illustrate accounts representing debt, let us select from the items in Fig. 6 some which imply indebtedness. Such are Nos. 1, 3, 4, 7, 8, 10 and 11. But of these there appear to be two groups. Nos. 1, 3 and 7 refer to dealings with A. B., to whom the subject of the narrative becomes indebted and discharges the debt. Let us take rather (as being nearest like a property account) Nos. 4, 8, 10 and 11, which represent C. D. as owing the person spoken of and as discharging his indebtedness. Obviously the current form of the account will be as follows:—

FIG. 10.
Account of the Indebtedness of C. D. to Me.

| Feb. 15 | Loaned in cash | $35 | | Apl. 10 | Repaid me | $10 |
| Mar. 5 | " " | 12 | | " 15 | " " | 20 |

or in its balanced form:

FIG. 11.
Account of the Indebtedness of C. D. to Me.

$35	$10
12	20
	Resultant 17
$47	$47

Again we have the same arrangement.

Increase of Indebtedness = Discharge of Indebtedness + Resultant, or Present Debt.

C. D. is called our Debtor. If we owed him he

would be our Creditor. By an extension of language, we call any discharge of his debt a *credit* also. Hence we can make a useful shortening of the title of the account by merely writing his name and, on the two sides, Debtor and Creditor respectively.

Fig 12.

Debtor.		C. D.		Creditor.

The separate items of the two sides are called *debits* and *credits*, and we give the equation still another form.

$$\text{Debits} = \text{Credits} + \textit{Net Debt}.$$

Now, considering the transactions with A. B., whereby we get into his debt and get out again, it may be observed that in the former he is truly creditor, and that it is usual to call the discharges of his creditorship *debits*. We may then write the title just as we did that of C. D., but the increase will be on the right-hand side, the decrease on the left.

Fig. 13.

Debtor.				A. B.			Creditor.
Feb. 2	Repaid him	$75		Jan. 1	Loaned me		$100
Mar. 3	" "	23					

The balancing of this account is on the same principle as heretofore, but the resultant is on the opposite side.

Fig. 14.

Dr.			A. B.		Cr.
		$75			$100
		23			
Resultant		2			
		$100			$100

THE GENERAL PRINCIPLES OF THE SCIENCE OF ACCOUNTS.*

A Course of Lectures delivered before the School of Commerce, Accounts and Finance, New York University, 1900-1901, by Col. Charles E. Sprague, A. M., Ph.D., C. P. A., President of the Union Dime Savings Institution.

Revised for Commerce, Accounts and Finance.

III. COMBINATION OF ACCOUNTS.

We have now constructed and balanced three simple accounts—one of property, one of a debt due us, one of a debt due from us. The former two are in our favor, the latter one is to our disadvantage.

We group together property and debts due us as Assets or Resources, being positive elements in our wealth. Debts due by us and from us are the negative elements, and we style them Liabilities.

Let us endeavor to assemble together these accounts or their resultants into an account of higher grade showing not transactions, but their results, the resulting status. The name of such an account is a *Balance Sheet.*

The amount of our wealth is the conclusion sought. Assets are positive elements. Liabilities are negative.

FIG. 14.
BALANCE SHEET.

Cash	$86	A. B.	$2
C, D.	17		

The resultant which will balance this account is variously known as Capital, Proprietorship, Worth, Stock, Estate. It is the excess of Asset over Liabilities, or the remainder which would exist if the liabilities were discharged by using up the necessary portion of the assets.

The Balance Sheet, when completed, is a Statement of the affairs of the proprietor.

FIG. 15.
BALANCE SHEET.

Cash	$86	A. B.	$2
C. D.	17	Proprietorship	101
	$103		$103

A Balance Sheet is, therefore, an account showing on one side the list of assets, and on the other the list of liabilities and the net amount of Proprietorship.

It will be noticed that three of the items in the Balance Sheet are resultants of accounts. The fourth might be so, likewise. In addition to accounts of Assets and Liabilities, we might have kept an account of Proprietorship. Upon re-examining the entries in Fig. 6, we find that some of them, while they express increase or decrease of cash, express also decrease or increase of proprietorship. No. 1 is not such an entry; while it is an increase of cash (assets), it is also a corresponding increase of liability. But in Nos. 2, 5, 6 and 9 there is an actual gain or loss in proprietorship.

If we make up an account from these items, it will produce the same resultant as before, $101.

FIG. 16.
PROPRIETORSHIP.

Jan 31	Rec'd Salary	$50	Mar. 1	Paid Expenses	$49
Feb 28	" "	50			
Mar 31	" "	50		*Resultant*	101
		$150			$150

THE GENERAL THEORY OF DOUBLE ENTRY.

1. An account must be kept for every asset or group of assets; increase on the left, decrease on the right.

2. An account must be kept for every liability or group of liabilities; increase on the right, decrease on the left.

3. If the assets are greater than the liabilities, an account (or accounts) must be kept for the proprietorship or capital; increase on the right, decerease on the left.

4. At any moment it must be true that

Assets = Liabilities + Capital.

5. Whenever desired, a Balance Sheet may be constructed, thus :—

Balance each account.

Carry the resultant to the opposite side of the balance sheet.

The balance sheet will then balance itself.

BALANCES.

Resultants which are thus carried to the balance sheet are called *balances.* We have not used the word heretofore, because frequently a resultant is merely to be transferred to some other account, not to the balance sheet; in such cases the word *balance* is not appropriate.

When, instead of keeping an account representing proprietorship, we merely kept those representing assets and liabilities, we were able to produce a statement, but this statement was not in equilibrium ; it did not balance. It was a Single Entry Statement. But when we employed a proprietorship account, the statement made up by combining all the resultants was itself in balance. That is the test of double entry bookkeeping. A double entry or complete system is one in which the balance sheet, being extracted from all the resultants, will of itself close and leave no residuum. Unless you can have that, you have not double entry bookkeeping.

"Single Entry Bookkeeping" is merely incomplete bookkeeping. It omits some, perhaps more, perhaps less, of the accounts which are necessary to a complete balance sheet.

DEBITS AND CREDITS.

Looking back over the four models of accounts which we have given—Cash, A. B., C. D. and Proprietorship—we see that the items composing them (exclusive of resultants) are of six kinds.

Increase of Assets	Decrease of Assets
Decrease of Liabilities	Increase of Liabilities
Decrease of Proprietorship	Increase of Proprietorship

The accounts of A. B. and C. D. representing indebtedness are called personal accounts, and they are the most numerous of all. We have seen that it is customary to head them on the two sides with "Debtor" and "Creditor," or, abbreviated, "Dr." and "Cr."; and to call the items on the left "debits" and those on the right "credits." By an extension of meaning, all items on the left-hand side of all accounts are known as "debits," and all on the right as "credits," although there be no reference to indebtedness.

Therefore, I give you the following rule for debits and credits, which I think is the best one for you, at least at the present stage :—

DEBITS, or entries on the lefthand side of the account are either:—

> More Assets.
> Less Liabilities, or
> Less Proprietorship.

CREDITS, or entries on the righthand side of the account, are either:—

> Less Assets.
> More Liabilities, or
> Greater Proprietorship.

"Less proprietorship" is usually expressed by "loss," and "greater proprietorship" by "gain" or "profit"; therefore we may express the rule in still another way :—

When we receive property
> we debit a property account.

When we part with property
> we credit a property account.

When we acquire a claim
> we debit a personal account.

When we relinquish a claim
> we credit a personal account.

When we incur an obligation
> we credit a personal account.

When we discharge an obligation
> we debit a personal account.

When we make a gain or increase our wealth
> we credit a proprietary account.

When we make a loss or diminish our wealth
> we debit a proprietary account.

THE GENERAL PRINCIPLES OF THE SCIENCE OF ACCOUNTS.*

A Course of Lectures delivered before the School of Commerce, Accounts and Finance, New York University, 1900-1901, by Col. Charles E. Sprague, A.M., Ph.D., C.P.A., President of the Union Dime Savings Institution.

Revised for Commerce, Accounts and Finance.

IV. THE BALANCE SHEET.

Speaking broadly, all accounts in the ledger exist for the sake of the balance sheet, and all other books and writings exist for the sake of the ledger. Therefore I continue to direct your attention to the balance sheet as the end and object of all else. As a matter of routine practice, the opposite order of presenting the subject would be preferable, and it is the usual one; namely, first to learn to make primary entries; then to analyze and journalize them; then to post them, and finally, after a very long apprenticeship at the keeping of accounts, to learn to construct a balance sheet.

But I am not here to teach you the craft of bookkeeping; I am to develop the principles of the science of accounts. From this point of view you must refer everything which is done to the balance sheet, and that must be constantly before your minds in regarding every process.

We might call the balance sheet the account of accounts, or the account of the status, or the account of the resultants. The balance sheet does not always contain the resultant of every separate account in the business, because, as I said, there are grades of accounts, and it may be that only certain higher grades are introduced into the balance sheet.

James Jones has the following resources and liabilities. We have derived this information either from his books or from observation and inventory. He has cash, $3,506.75; merchandise, $22,166.73; he has due from various personal debtors, $15,972.18; real estate, $10,000.00; he owes a mortgage, or there is a mortgage on his real estate, of $4,000.00; he owes to various personal creditors $18,718.62.

We can readily obtain what his proprietorship or capital is from that statement, but I call your attention to the following: We say, "Due from various personal debtors, $15,972.18." Well, now, if that be the only account kept with those personal debtors, it is very difficult to tell what any one personal debtor owes him, and it would be rather a difficult search to ascertain. Presumably there is a separate account kept in the first instance with each individual debtor; then there is a higher grade of account which considers the entire body of debtors as a unit, and at any moment answers the question, "How much is due from all our debtors in the aggregate?" Possibly this higher grade of account would not be formally kept, but there would have to be a list somewhere from which the amount of the aggregate indebtedness from each personal debtor would be combined and brought into this one single sum. There would have to be, either formally or explicitly, an intermediate account, an account between the balance sheet and the individual debtors' account. So we may have several grades, but we seldom go beyond the third grade. We must necessarily have the balance sheet as the highest account; the condensed balance sheet, condensed to such degree as the business may require, and then we must have somewhere an account, either in form or else in substance, for each item of the balance sheet; and

finally, for each *complex* item of the balance sheet, which represents a group of persons or things of the same character, subordinate accounts, usually kept in subordinate ledgers. Thus, by these different grades of accounts, we accomplish the double requirement of minute information as to details and comprehensive information as to broad results.

The group account, or the list of "personal debtors," would itself be a sort of balance sheet of the subordinate system of separate accounts, and a check upon its accuracy. You will find by experience that such a group account will save more time than it consumes.

Let us write out a statement of James Jones's affairs, but this time let us do so in two ways, one as before, with the assets to the left of the liabilities; the other with the liabilities on the left. In both forms let us head the two sides Dr. and Cr., just similarly, and let us examine how those terms apply.

In No. 1 consider the personal debtors; they are on the debtor side because *they* owe *Jones*; in No. 2 they are on the creditor side, hence in this form we are emphasizing the fact that *Jones* is the *creditor*.

It would seem then that in the former case, No. 1, we expressed the relations of all *other* people towards Jones; in the latter case, No. 2, it is the relation (if any) of *Jones* to every one else. Grammatically speaking, in form No. 1 Jones is the object of the verb "owes" or "trusts," while in form No. 2 he is the subject.

If this is true, it will apply also to the liabilities, and we find this to be the case. In form No. 2 Jones's creditors are on the debtor side, because he, the subject of the account, *is* debtor, and in No. 1 *they*, being creditors, are on the credit side.

Once more, we can apply this reasoning to the property accounts? Can they be said to be *debtor or creditor?* Not in the ordinary sense of the word. We must again extend the use of the words "Debtor" and "Creditor" in precisely the same manner as we have extended the words "debit" and "credit" in speaking of items. You remember that we agreed that "debits" should mean not only debts but increase of property. So let us agree that "Dr." shall mean not only literally "debtor," but when speaking of property shall mean "belonging to," "the property of;" and that "Cr." shall mean "owner of," "possessor of." With this extended meaning, "Cash Dr. to James Jones" is no longer an absurdity; it means nothing about owing, but that there is $3,506.75 *belonging to* Jones. "James Jones, Cr. by Cash," also becomes entirely rational; it means Jones is the *owner of* $3,506.75.

We are now prepared to make up these balance sheets and to head them understandingly.

FIG. 17—No. 1

Balance Sheet of James Jones [Relations of persons and property to him]			
Dr. [Debtors owing him or property belonging to him]		Cr. [Creditors claiming from him, or his actual ownership]	
Cash	$3,506.75	Mortgage	$4,000.00
Merchandise	22,166.73		
Personal Debtors	15,972.15		
Real Estate	10,000.00	*James Jones*	47,645.63
	$51,645.63		$51,645.63

Dr.	James Jones		Cr.
	[*his* relations to persons and property]		
[Showing how *he* is indebted]			[Showing how *he* is creditor or owner]
Mortgage Payable $4,000.00	Cash	$3,506.75	
	Merchandise	22,166.73	
	Personal Debtors	15,972.15	
	Real Estate	10,000.00	
$4,000.00		$51,645.63	
	James Jones [net owner]	$47,645.63	

We have here reduced Jones's proprietary account by the method of Figure 7—by the method of simple subtraction. We might have done so by the balance or scale method shown in Figs. 8 and 9.

Dr.	James Jones		Cr.
Mortgage Payable $4,000.00	Cash	$3,506.75	
	Merchandise	22,166.73	
	Personal Debtors	15,972.15	
Net Capital 47,645.63	Real Estate	10,000.00	
$51,645.63		$51,645.63	

The second arrangement of the balance sheet—the one which places the assets on the right—is little used, except in England, and even there not universally. The other arrangement—debtors on the debit side and creditors on the credit side—seems to us by far more natural and intelligible.

When we say "in account with" between two names, the meaning is this: *A in account with B*, means that A is represented as debtor and creditor, according to the facts, while *B in account with A* means that the same facts are represented on the opposite sides and from the converse point of view, since each must be debtor when the other is creditor.

With this understanding we may designate the two forms of balance sheet thus:

THE UNIVERSE IN A/C WITH JONES

or

JONES IN A/C WITH THE UNIVERSE.

In non-English speaking countries it is usual to head balance sheets, not Dr. and Cr., but ACTIVE & PASSIVE.

THE GENERAL PRINCIPLES OF THE SCIENCE OF ACCOUNTS.*

A Course of Lectures delivered before the School of Commerce,
Accounts and Finance, New York University, 1900-1901,
by Col. Charles E. Sprague, A.M., Ph.D., C.P.A.,
President of the Union Dime Savings Institution.

Revised for Commerce, Accounts and Finance.

V.—A PARTNERSHIP BALANCE SHEET.

We have so far considered the simplest form of proprietorship, that of a single proprietor. When two or more persons form a partnership, they become jointly *debtors* for the liabilities, and *creditors* (in the extended sense) for the assets.

We may suppose that James Jones, having the status shown by the foregoing balance sheet, forms a partnership, taking in William Smith, whose balance sheet is as follows:—

FIG. 18

Balance Sheet of William Smith

Cash	$5,082.34	Bills Payable	$3,000.00
Merchandise	17,082.65	Personal Creditors	5,465.35
Personal Debtors	8,123.17		
Bills Receivable	7,000.00	*William Smith*	23,822.81
	$37,288.16		$37,288.16

Let us combine the two balance sheets into one. The two cash balances will be united into the firm's cash; the merchandise is now owned jointly, the partners are jointly liable for the debts, and so on through the list. Adding together all the amounts of like components, we get the following balance sheet:—

FIG. 19

Balance Sheet of Jones & Smith

Cash	$8,589.09	Bills Payable	$8,000.00
Merchandise	39,249.38	Personal Creditors	5,465.35
Bills Receivable	7,000.00	Mortgage Payable	4,000.00
Personal Debtors	24,095.32	*Jones & Smith*	
Real Estate	10,000.00	*(joint capital)*	71,468.44
	$88,933.79		$88,933.79

But it may be desirable to retain a separate account of the capital of each partner, in which case the balance sheet would take this form:—

FIG. 20

Balance Sheet of Jones & Smith

Cash	$8,589.09	Bills Payable	$8,000.00
Merchandise	39,249.38	Personal Creditors	5,465.35
Bills Receivable	7,000.00	Mortgages Payable	4,000.00
Personal Debtors	24,095.32	*James Jones*	47,645.63
Real Estate	10,000.00	*William Smith*	23,822.81
	$88,933.79		$88,933.79

The circumstances of each particular case would indicate which of these forms to select. For example,

* Copyright, 1901, by the Accounting Press.

it might or might not be desirable, in submitting a balance sheet for the purpose of establishing credit, to make known the fact that Mr. Jones is owner of two-thirds and Mr. Smith of one-third only.

CORPORATE BALANCE SHEET.

Still another form of complex proprietorship arises from the formation of companies or corporations instead of partnerships. Here it is usual to have a fixed amount of capital, divided into convenient-sized shares, and, in theory at least, this is approximately the amount of the actual proprietorship.

Let it be supposed that Messrs. Jones & Smith, instead of a partnership, had preferred to form a company, named the Jones Mercantile Company. They consider that, as the actual value of their joint proprietorship is over $71,000, it would be quite proper to capitalize it at $60,000, in 600 shares, of $100 each. Nevertheless, there is a total proprietorship of $71,468.44, as before, all of which must be represented in some form.

In order to represent both the amount of the capitalization and the true proprietary value, we divide the total proprietorship into two parts:—

1.	Capital; par, or face value of shares	$60,000.00
2.	Surplus; excess of real value over par	11,468.44
	Their sum is the real proprietorship	$71,468.44

The resulting balance sheet would be:—

FIG. 21

Balance Sheet of the Jones Mercantile Company

Cash	$8,589.09	Bills Payable	$8,000.00
Merchandise	39,249.38	Personal Creditors	5,465.35
Bills Receivable	7,000.00	Mortgage Payable	4,000.00
Personal Debtors	24,095.32	*Capital Stock*	60,000.00
Real Estate	10,000.00	*Surplus*	11,468.44
	$88,933.79		$88,933.79

The value of each share would be:—

$$\$71,468.44 \div 600 = \$119.11 +$$

Perhaps (and this is often the case) the capitalization at $75,000 would be preferred, as nearer the true figure—750 shares instead of 600. The construction of the balance sheet is not so easy in this case, as the item corresponding to Surplus must be on the other side.

FIG. 22

Balance Sheet of the Jones Mercantile Company

Cash	$8,589.09	Bills Payable	$8,000.00
Merchandise	39,249.38	Personal Creditors	5,465.35
Bills Receivable	7,000.00	Mortgage Payable	4,000.00
Personal Debtors	24,095.32		
Real Estate	10,000.00		
[..............]?	3,531.56	*Capital Stock*	75,000.00
	$92,465.35		$92,465.35

What shall we call the item $3,531.56? There is a strange reluctance to name it "Deficit," "Discount," "Water" or any name implying that the capital stock is worth less than par. A deficiency is usually veiled, while a surplus is unblushingly avowed. Rather than confess that this item is an offset to the value of the capital stock, it is customary to label it as an actual asset, usually of so intangible a nature and so indeterminate value that its existence is purely a matter of opinion. "Good Will" is such a title much used (and often with good reason) in mercantile enterprises; "Franchise" for corporations utilizing some public rights or property; "Patents" for companies using some inventions. These are frequently valid assets, but their value is almost necessarily conjectural.

ORDER OF THE BALANCE SHEET.

It will be noticed that in all the examples of the balance sheet which we have presented, the assets have commenced with "Cash." The general rule followed has been to begin with the most available assets and the most pressing liabilities. Many balance sheets do not obey this rule; in fact, they do not seem to be arranged on any definite plan whatever, but to be placed at haphazard.

[The construction and interpretation of a balance sheet were illustrated by exhibiting the statement of a trust company (1) in the conventional form, (2) as printed in an analytical form for the information of depositors. In the latter form the debits began with "Cash," and the credits ended with "Capital and Surplus"; just the reverse being true in the first form.]

OPENING OR RE-OPENING ACCOUNTS.

We have seen that the balance-sheet is a recapitulation of the results of the accounts, if accounts have been kept; but, in any case, it is an account of the status of an individual or a concern at some definite moment. It is not a suitable form for expressing the current changes which take place in some or all of the components; for this purpose we must return to the form of separate accounts constituting the ledger.

Each amount or balance in the balance sheet is used to inaugurate or "open" an account in the ledger, on the same side. If the accounts are to continue in the same books, the re-opening balance will appear under the double lines which have indicated the closure.

Thus the four little accounts in Figs. 9, 11, 14 and 16, which were closed into a Balance Sheet at Fig. 15, may be re-opened by distributing the items, or balances as we now call them, into the old "frames." In reproducing them we will insert opposite each entry the name of the account where its converse appears, prefixing the prepositions "To" and "By," which are of no special utility, as the side of the account is quite as distinctive, to say nothing of the abbreviations "Dr." and "Cr.," which, in deference to custom, we will also place over the accounts.

FIG. 23

Dr		Cash			Cr
Jan. 1	To A. B.	$100	Feb. 2	By A. B.	$75
" 31	" Proprietor	50	" 15	" C. D.	35
Feb. 28	" Proprietor	50	Mar. 1	" Proprietor	49
Mar. 31	" Proprietor	50	" 3	" A. B.	23
Apl. 10	" C. D.	10	" 5	" C. D.	12
" 15	" C. D.	20	Apl 30	" Balance	86
		$280			$280
May 1	To Balance	$86			

Dr		C. D.			Cr
Feb. 15	To Cash	$35	Apl. 10	By Cash	$10
Mar. 5	" "	12	" 15	" "	20
			" 30	" Balance	17
		$47			
May 1	To Balance	$17			

Dr		A. B.			Cr
Feb. 2	To Cash	$75	Jan. 1	By Cash	$100
Mar. 3	" "	23			
Apl. 30	" Balance	2			
		$100			$100
			May 1	By Balance	$2

Dr		Proprietor			Cr
Mar. 1	To Cash	$49	Jan. 31	By Cash	$50
Apl. 30	" Balance	101	Feb. 28	" "	50
			Mar. 31	" "	50
		$150			$150
			May 1	By Balance	$101

BRINGING DOWN BALANCES.

If we look at the Cash account, Fig. 23, in its present state, we see that the process of carrying its resultant into the Balance Sheet and bringing it back has had the effect of simply reducing it to a single term—the same effect as that of the process in Fig. 7. In fact, a break, or stop, in an account is frequently made in this way, without reference to any balance sheet or balancing period. On the other hand, the ceremony of inserting the balance on each side is frequently omitted, the figures being extracted for the purpose without disturbing the current record.

THE ANCIENT BALANCE ACCOUNT.

Formerly, when there was but one source of entries, the journal—and nothing could be introduced into the ledger except from the journal—the theory of the balance sheet was more symmetrical than now, but at the same time more cumbersome. The historical development was as follows:—

1. The Balance Accounts were part of the ledger, like any other accounts, and there were two, "Entering Balance" and "Exit Balance" (Balance d'Entrée, Balance de Sortie). By journal entries (which will be hereafter explained) the balance of every account was transferred to the "Exit Balance" account, each account being ruled off as if it actually balanced of itself. The "Exit Balance" thus is put in equilibrium, and itself ruled off. Next another series of journal entries of opposite character debiting and crediting "Entering Balances" was put in operation, whereby the balances are restored below the double lines. The "Entering Balance" account is self-closed.

2. The first abbreviation is to have only one "Balance Account," which takes the form of the "Exit Balance." The "Entering Balance" account is omitted, but the balance of each account is separately "brought down" to the opposite side.

3. The Balance is no longer considered a ledger ac-

count, but as something outside of the system. The accounts are balanced and brought down at the same process, and the Balance Sheet is a list or transcript of the balances, taken in passing.

4. The process of balancing each account at the moment of taking the Balance Sheet is not insisted upon, but the amount of the balance is ascertained in any convenient way, and inserted in the Balance Sheet, which may leave no permanent trace by which it may be verified.

The tendency of modern accounting is towards form No. 4, which finds its extreme development in the ledger, with a balance column keeping the balance perpetually in sight. In this case those balances which are to figure in the balance sheet are marked in some way, to distinguish them from others.

THE GENERAL PRINCIPLES OF THE SCIENCE OF ACCOUNTS.*

A Course of Lectures delivered before the School of Commerce, Accounts and Finance, New York University, 1900-1901, by Col. Charles E. Sprague, A. M., Ph.D., C. P. A., President of the Union Dime Savings Institution.

Revised for Commerce, Accounts and Finance.

VI.—THE TRANSACTION.

We have thus considered the account in two ways, tracing it up to the balance sheet and down to the item. We must now go a step further and analyze the transactions from which the items of account are derived.

It becomes evident upon examination of any financial or business transaction that it must affect at least two accounts and in opposite ways. For if there is an exchange of property or indebtedness, or both, there must necessarily be more than one account affected; while if, instead of an exchange, there is a giving or receiving, or an indebtedness, without equivalent, then a proprietary account of some kind must be affected.

The few transactions already given (in Lecture II.) were there introduced as items of a cash account; but we afterward found that each of them gave rise also to an item of some other account representing indebtedness or else proprietorship.

We shall now introduce a series of very simple transactions which we shall analyze or distribute into debits and credits, showing what accounts are affected and that the equilibrium is not thereby disturbed.

I shall take the case of a young man who has nothing and owes nothing, whose balance sheet is a zero on both sides. I am going to suppose that Stephen Steady borrows twenty-five dollars from his father, Hiram Steady, with which to seek his fortune in the city, from January 1st, and he commences keeping a diary of his financial transactions as follows:—

(a) Stephen Steady borrows $25, from his father,

William Steady, with which to seek his fortune in the city, January 1, 1882. His diary is as follows:—

(b) January 2. Paid for railroad fare, $4.65; (c) for lunch, 30 cents; (d) for hotel bill, $1.

(e) January 3. Engaged board with Mrs. Malone at $4.50 per week. Paid one week's board in advance. (f) Deposited $10 in the City Savings Bank.

January 4. Obtained employment with Messrs. Cheeryble Brothers at $12 per week.

(g) January 11. Received from Cheeryble Brothers one week's wages, $12.

(h) January 12. Sent my father $5 to apply on loan.

(i) January 13. Lent Fred Watson $4.

(j) January 17. One week's board ending today, $4.50.

(k) January 18. One week's wages, $12. (l) Sent my father $6; (m) deposited $3.

(n) January 20. Fred Watson repaid me $3; (o) drew from the bank $4.

(p) January 23. Purchased an overcoat, $8.50; (q) a pair of shoes, $3.

Transaction (a). Cash increased, but a corresponding liability created.

Increase of assets.......................Cash, Dr.
Increase of liabilities ....Hiram Steady, Cr.

These two items arising from the transaction are generally expressed as follows:—

"Cash, Dr.. $25.00
To Hiram Steady, $25.00
for money borrowed."

In this form it is called a journal entry or the entry of the transaction. The following forms are also in use:—

Form 2.
Cash | Hiram Steady $25.00 $25.00
for money loaned.

Form 3.

Date	For what	Amount Dr.	Account Dr.	Account Cr.	Amount Dr.
Jan. 1	Money loaned	$25 00	Cash	H. Steady	$25 00

(b) Paid for railroad fare, $4.65. When the ticket has been taken up, there is no equivalent for this decrease of assets; nothing tangible is received in return nor is any liability cancelled. Simon's financial thermometer is below zero. It is a decrease of his proprietorship.

Decrease of assets......................Cash, Cr.
Decrease of Proprietorship.......Simon Steady, Dr.

Here comes a peculiarity of the proprietorship account. It is seldom desirable to enter at once in the proprietorship account every little accretion or diminution, because while that would give minuteness, which is one of the requisites of information in accounts, it would not give comprehensiveness. Therefore, to gain comprehensiveness, while obtaining minuteness, it will be best, temporarily, to keep separate those items or transactions which cause an increase or decrease of the total wealth of Mr. Steady. This is done by using temporary accounts, which are really subdivisions of Proprietorship. They represent Outlay and Income in various forms; sometimes all in one account; sometimes all outlay in one account, and all income in another; sometimes each account represents only some one branch of outlay or of income. For the purpose of this analysis we will open only one account for all outlay and all income and will call it Profit and Loss. Some object to this title, preferring the order Loss and Profit, or Loss and Gain, in order not to have the word "Profit" stand above the losses and the word "Loss" above the profits.

The entry will then be :—
   "Profit & Loss | Cash $4.65 $4.65
for car fare."

(c) (d) These entries are of precisely the same nature.

(e) is of the same nature, except that, as the board is paid in advance, there is actually not an outlay for the moment, but Mrs. Malone is indebted for the amount. But practically this may be disregarded, as there is no danger that Simon will forget to eat his meals and thus collect the debt.

(f) Deposited in the City Savings Bank, $10. This is a decrease of one asset, cash, and an increase of another. Whether we consider the deposit as *something* which we own, or the bank as *some one* who owes us; whether this new element in Steady's "active" is property or a debt receivable, does not matter; it is in either case an asset. The entry will be.

City Savings Bank | Cash $10.00 $10.00
for deposit.

On January 4th Mr. Steady had the good fortune to obtain employment with the eminent firm of Messrs. Cheeryble Brothers at $12 a week, and at the end of the week, January 11th, he received from them one week's wages, $12. In his limited method of bookkeeping, the recording of that contract as a liability on the part of Messrs. Cheeryble Brothers is not necessary; but the fact that he received $12, a week's wages, on January 11th, is important.

(g) Increase of proprietorship with increase of assets.

"Cash | Profit & Loss $12.00 $12.00
for one week's wages to Jan. 11."

(h) Here is the decrease of an asset (cash) with the partial cancellation of a liability.

   Hiram Steady | Cash $5.00 $5.00
for payment on account loan.

POSTING.

It will be easy to frame four accounts—Cash, Hiram Steady, City Savings Bank and Profit and Loss—and to *post* them by writing each item of each transaction to the proper side of the proper account. [Illustrated on blackboard.]

THE TRIAL BALANCE.

As each transaction has been shown to give an equal amount of debit and credit, the aggregate of all the transactions, or, in other words, the aggregates of all the accounts, must also contain an equal amount of debit and of credit, *if the accounts have been correctly kept.*

As a test of correctness, therefore, a list of all the accounts is made, and this list, which is called a Trial Balance, must itself be in equilibrium. If it is not, there is surely some error; if it is, there *may* be double or counterbalancing errors.

The following is a trial balance taken at this point :—

FIG. 24.

Dr.	Trial Balance.	Cr.
$37	Cash	$25 45
5	Hiram Steady	25
10	City Savings Bank	
10 45	Profit and Loss	12
$62 45		$62 45

No error is discovered. The total, $62.45, is also the total of the original transactions, as might have been ascertained by making a list of them.

The resultants of the accounts might have been used instead of the totals of both sides, thus :—

FIG. 25.

Dr.	Trial Balance.	Cr.
$11 55	Cash	
	Hiram Steady	$20 00
10 00	City Savings Bank	
	Profit and Loss	1 55
$21 55		$21 55

This, however, is in most cases a less useful test than the previous form, as it would not detect the failure to post an entire transaction.

ANALYSIS OF TRANSACTIONS RESUMED.

(i) Lent Fred Watson $4. This introduces a new account, one of indebtedness active.

   Increase of Assets (Fred Watson, Dr.).
      Decrease of Assets (Cash, Cr.).

(j) (k) (l) and (m) present nothing new.
(n) is the converse of (i).
(o) is the converse of (f).
(p) and (q) may be treated in either of two ways. If the overcoat and the shoes are considered as property, an account would have to be opened for that

class of property. If they are considered as mere expenditure or consumption, then Profit and Loss would simply be debited. In the long run, however, these articles are destined to be consumed, and not to be disposed of in any other way. Considered as property, there would be an instantaneous depreciation difficult to measure, from the mere fact of their being second-hand.

But in either case the entry would be to credit cash and to debit some account representing the equivalent either as property or as outlay. This illustrates a frequently occurring class of entries where the *side* of the item is perfectly certain, although it is doubtful as to whether it refers to property, indebtedness or wealth. Thus if we had an account entitled "Wearing Apparel" to which such purchases were posted, we need not trouble ourselves as to whether this account represents property or loss of wealth; the debit will be as surely correct in one case as the other. We can wait till the next time of balancing to determine deliberately whether this is property, or merely loss, or (which is more likely) partly one and partly the other.

For simplicity, let us consider these transactions as pure outlay and the entry as

Profit and Loss | Cash.

ADJUSTMENT.

It is required to take a balance sheet of Simon Steady's affairs under date of January 24th.

Going through the familiar process of constructing the balance sheet, it is found that he appears to be worth less than nothing, although he has worked seventeen working days at $2, and has only spent $26.45. Investigating this, it is further found that, although he has worked seventeen days, he has only been paid for twelve, pay-day being tomorrow. The five days' work have been performed, and, although Cheeryble Brothers do not yet have to pay it, yet Steady is entitled to its value as an asset.

This adjustment may be made by opening an account with Cheeryble Brothers, or a property account under some such title as "Wages Receivable" or "Accrued Wages."

This gives rise to a new type of entry, not exactly of a transaction, but of an adjustment. In this case it would involve an increase of assets and an increase of proprietorship.

(r) Accrued Wages | Profit and Loss $10.00 | $10.00

Care must be taken, when the next week's wages is paid, only to credit $2 to Profit and Loss, $10 going to the credit of Accrued Wages. The $10 had already been recorded as earned, and must not again be so recorded.

In the same manner, looking over the items of the Profit and Loss account to see if any other outlay or income requires adjustment, we find that Steady has consumed Mrs. Malone's food and used her room for a week without payment. This must be adjusted likewise. But the board bill is not merely accrued; it is due and payable, and constitutes a liability. This is an outlay, not in cash, but in the creation of a liability, and will constitute entry (r):—

Profit and Loss | Mrs. Malone $4.50 | $4.50

ADJUSTMENTS.

Adjustment entries usually arise from the fact that expense and revenue gradually *accrue* from day to day, while they *mature*, or become payable, at convenient periods, and, finally (either promptly or otherwise), are *paid*. Thus the earning and collection of revenue are continually falling into three stages. Take house rent as an example, payable monthly on the last day.

1. The rent from day to day, as earned and accruing, is an asset—RENT ACCRUED.

2. When the end of the month arrives it is still an asset, but is now a personal indebtedness of the tenant.

3. When actually paid it vanishes as an asset, having been converted into cash.

The earning of the rent may be recorded in either of three ways. Let *Rent-Earnings* be the title of an account subsidiary to Profit and Loss and devoted to this particular kind of earnings. Then the three methods are as follows:—

1. The rent earned each day is recorded each day by the entry:—

Rent Accrued | Rent Earnings.

At the stipulated period the rent accrued is transferred to the account of rent due, which is a personal claim demandable from the several tenants. Entry:—

Rent Due | Rent Accrued.

When collected the entry is:—

Cash | Rent Due.

2. In this method no attention is paid to the rent accruing daily, but at the stipulated period the entry is:—

Rent Due | Rent Earnings.

and when collected:—

Cash | Rent Due.

3. In this method no attention is paid either to the accruing or the maturing of the rent, but the one entry is made at collecton:—

Cash | Rent Earnings.

It is obvious that the first method will not require adjustment at any time; that the second will require adjustment if the balancing period and the rent period do not coincide; that the third will require adjustment unless all rent happens to have been collected up to the very day of balancing and none beyond.

Adjustment will also be requisite in accounts of expenditure for things gradually consumed. Coal for use of the engine may be first delivered, then paid for, then gradually consumed. It is not the delivery nor the payment which lessens the proprietor's wealth, but the consumption; though we may roughly, for current convenience, charge it as outlay when delivered or when paid for. If we do this, we must not omit to adjust the account at the time of balancing, so as to divide the coal consumed from the coal unconsumed, the former being a vanishing of capital, the latter an asset.

The word "Rent" is more frequently used than "Rent-Earnings." I have here employed this latter word purposely to differentiate two things which are often confused by bookkeepers. "Rent" or "Interest" is often the title of an account where it is difficult to see whether the conclusion sought is, "How much is due me for rent?" or "How much have I benefited by earnings from rent?" The two may be mingled together in one account—any two accounts *may* be mingled together; but it is clearer to keep them separate.

The General Principles of the Science of Accounts*

A Course of Lectures delivered before the School of Commerce, Accounts and Finance, New York University, 1900-1901, by Col. Charles E. Sprague, A. M., Ph.D., C.P.A., President of the Union Dime Savings Institution.

Revised for Commerce, Accounts and Finance.

VII.—SPECIFIC AND ECONOMIC ACCOUNTS

Having made up a miniature ledger from the entries which we have been discussing, we find the following balances, which reveal the status of Simon Steady's affairs:—

Cash	$1.55	Hiram Steady	$14.00
Accrued wages	10.00	Mrs. Malone	4.50
City savings bank	9.00		
Fred Watson	1.00		

This is a *specific* statement of the affairs; it tells us in what things his wealth is invested and subject to what liabilities. It does not, however, tell the source of this wealth.

Take the remaining element of the balance sheet, which is simply:—

Profit and Loss, $3.05.

This gives a statement of the amount of proprietorship and shows that its source is earnings, but does not give the least hint of what things compose the proprietorship.

But looked at as a statement of source, it is not sufficiently subdivided. We must go back to the account of which it is a resultant in order to ascertain by what forces and causes the present conditions have been reached.

Let us substitute for the Profit and Loss the following account: Wages, Board, Clothing and Miscellaneous Expenses.

FIG. 26
Wages

(g)		$12.00
(k)		12.00
(r)		10.00

Board

(e)		$4.50
(j)		4.50
(s)		4.50

Clothing

(p)		$8.50
(q)		3.00

Miscellaneous Expense

(b)		$4.65
(c)		.30
(d)		1.00

We might use the resultants of these four accounts as an *economic* statement, showing analytically the sources of the $3.05. If we placed them directly in the balance sheet and then divided the latter into two groups, we should have this result:—

FIG. 27
Balance Sheet

1 Specific Accounts. (Net Assets, $3.05)					
Specific Accounts. (Net Assets, $3.05)	Cash	$1	55	Hiram Steady	$14	00
	Accrued Wages	10	00	Mrs. Malone	4	50
	City Savings Bk	9	00			
	Fred Watson	1	00			
2 Economic Accounts. (Net Proprietorship, $3.05)	Board	13	50	Wages	34	00
	Clothing	11	50			
	Misc. Expense	5	95			
		$52	50		$52	50

Thus we get a new classification of accounts, the *specific*, showing *what*, the *economic*, *whence* or *why*.

Thus, by the device of subordinate accounts, we make the main proprietary accounts clearer by relieving them of a mass of daily increments and decrements. We assume a certain portion of time, say the year, as the fiscal period, and agree to let all business increments and decrements during that period be kept out of the capital accounts. We therefore open a "Profit and Loss" or "Loss and Gain" or

"Outlay and Income" account, whose function it shall be to furnish a systematic statement of the success of the business *during the period*. Mixing it up with a balance brought forward and a balance carried forward, I think, obscures it.

Profit and loss always relates, or usually relates, to some definite period of time. We arrest the proprietorship account proper; we halt right there and let all increases and decreases of it be treasured up into a reservoir which we call profit and loss account. But generally we are not even satisfied with that. We provide a number of lesser reservoirs or cells, because it is necessary to analyze more closely the sources of income and the purposes of outlay. Therefore, a profit and loss account alone is impracticable. We found it practicable with little Stephen Steady's accounts here, but we should not with anything of more magnitude. We must have the different sources of income separated. We must have different objects of expense separated in order that we may know in what way we are getting ahead and in what way we are getting behind; whether we have expended too much, or whether we have not received enough. Profit and loss account is subordinate to proprietorship account. It is proprietorship in transit, in fluctuation, but profit and loss itself is too broad, and usually there are subdivisions of both sides of it.

But extraordinary circumstances other than the normal outlay and income of the business find their way into capital accounts more directly by a sort of short-circuiting. If a man suddenly receives an access of capital by inheritance, that is not profit and loss; that is a direct increase of his proprietorship by a cause that is totally independent of his exertions and of his success or failure in the business. The Italian writers call that a *supervenience*, which is a very awkward word in English. It would be well if we had something like that, an expression meaning a coming-upon. I have thought that the word *occurrences* would be good. That is a little too broad, but it is a coming upon the proprietor of something that is outside of his earnings from the business.

That is one grade. Now the profit and loss account may have some incidental occurrences of that kind, some superveniences into profit and loss account. There may be some extraordinary and abnormal gains, not like these inheritances, which are not gain at all, but which are mere accretion; or, rather, they are not an accretion, which means a growing on, but they are a coming on, a supervenience; we may have an abnormal profit or loss in the business which does not fit into the ordinary classification. It is a good fortune or it is a misfortune. It is quite proper to put that directly under profit and loss account. Having entered any extraordinary superveniences of capital directly in the proprietorship account, and having entered any extraordinary gains or losses in the profit and loss account, all the normal benefits or adversities of the outlay and of the income of the business are distributed in the accounts subordinate to profit and loss, merely as temporary reservoirs or buckets into which they are to be placed in order to keep them separate. It is perfectly easy to mix things together if you have kept them separate; but it is not so easy to disentangle them after you throw them all together. It is a proverb that anybody can mix wine and water, but nobody in the world can separate them after they are mixed. It is best on the whole to divide too much rather than too little, because you can always put things together, if you decide that they are too much separated.

Now, at the close of the fiscal period, our economic accounts are in the following state: The Capital or Proprietary accounts contain merely their initial balances, unchanged save for any special superveniences; the Profit and Loss account contains only abnormal or supervenient losses and gains during the period; while the true economic history is scattered in various accounts subordinate to, or portions of, Profit and Loss.

Manifestly these must be united. First, each subordinate account must be adjusted, that is, the inaccuracies which result from the overlappings of time, etc., and which in the current state of the accounts can be disregarded, must be corrected. Then the minor economic accounts are closed into the Profit and Loss account, which thus becomes an analysis, answering the question, "How did you get here?" For example:—

FIG. 28
Profit and Loss

Board	$13	50	Wages	$34	00
Clothing	11	50			
Misc. Expense	5	95			
To Capital	*3*	*05*			
	$34	00		$34	00

This result is carried to Capital account.

FIG. 28
Simon Steady

Balance	$3	05	....	....	..
			Profit and Loss	$3	05
	$3	05		$3	05

And the Balance Sheet corroborates it.

FIG. 29
Balance Sheet

Cash	$1	55	Hiram Steady	$14	00
Accrued Wages	10	00	Mrs. Malone	4	50
City Savings Bk	9	00			
Fred Watson	1	00	*Simon Steady*	*3*	*05*
	$21	55		$21	55

This gives us another view of the functions of double-entry accounts, obtaining the present status by two methods, the specific accounts, showing in what it consists; the economic accounts, showing how it has been produced; both centering in the proprietary accounts and proving each other.

The General Principles of the Science of Accounts*

A Course of Lectures delivered before the School of Commerce, Accounts and Finance, New York University, 1900-1901, by Col. Charles E. Sprague, A. M., Ph.D., C.P.A., President of the Union Dime Savings Institution.

Revised for Commerce, Accounts and Finance.

MIXED ACCOUNTS—SPECIFIC ECONOMICS.

In the classification of accounts—in fact, in almost any kind of classification—there will be some things either so near the border line of two classes that it is doubtful where to place them, or partaking of the qualities of both to such an extent as to be really of a two-fold nature.

A good example of such an account is the Merchandise Account, in the form still prevalent but gradually being disused.

Merchandise is something bought at a certain cost-price, for the purpose of selling at another price. The latter price consists of two parts—one equal to the cost, which it repays, the other the Merchandise-Profit, which is earned by services in bringing the goods near the customer, in selecting them with reference to their desirable qualities, in providing a convenient place where they may be examined and compared, and in always holding enough in stock to meet all reasonable demands.

Viewed in this light, every sale is properly creditable to two accounts, one to the Asset Merchandise parted with, the other to the Income Account, Profit.

But it seems to be considered impracticable in retail business, even on a large scale, to separate each sale into its two elements, and to know at each transaction how much goes to replace the goods and how much to pay the dealer for services, risk and expense. One would suppose it feasible, and some merchants have found it so, to record in a column of the salesbook the original cost of each article. But more usually the sale-price is undivided.

The Merchandise Account, therefore, becomes a

mixed account. On the debit side it contains entries at cost-price, and on the credit side at selling-price. There is no correlation revealed between the two sets of values; they might as well be in rupees and reichsmarks.

Hence some writers have, in their zeal for classification, considered the Merchandise Account as purely an Outlay and Income Account. The merchandise is not considered as property, but rather a mere form of cash expenditure, to be recouped ultimately by receipts of greater amount. The resultant is profit. But the difficulty arises when we consider that the merchandise on hand *is* property of too great value to be ignored. The way to get over this difficulty is to consider the merchandise on hand at the balancing period as an adjustment—an offset to the purchases.

Other authors again would classify this account as strictly a specific account—an asset. The difficulty here is that if we attempt to balance such an account we get a false balance, corresponding to nothing. Hence the canon prevails that there is a increment of value to the extent of the profit; that the merchandise purchased has, so far as sold, appreciated to that extent.

But whether the Merchandise Account be regarded as specific, or economic, or, as I contend, mixed, the calculation and the recording of the resultants are substantially the same. Let us take as an example the following facts:—

Mdse. on hand January 1.........................$5,643.75
Bought during January........................... 2,644.18
Sold during January............................. 3,219.74
Bought during February.......................... 1,845.17
Sold during February............................ 2,454.62
Bought during March............................. 1,929.44
Sold during March............................... 1,728.96

From these data let us construct an account.

FIG. 30
Merchandise

Jan. 1	Balance	$5,643.75			
"	Purchases	2,644.18	Jan.	Sales	$3,219.74
Feb.	"	1,845.17	Feb.	"	2,454.62
March	"	1,929.44	March	"	1,728.96

But from this we can draw no conclusion. The debit side amounts to $12,062.54, and the credit side to \$7,403.32, but the difference, \$4,659.22, is not an asset, for that would be assuming that we have sold at cost price, and it cannot be a loss, for that would be assuming that there is no balance remaining. If we know the profit, we can ascertain the balance; if we know the balance we can ascertain the profit.

The balance on hand, ascertained by *inventory*, taken at cost price, is the key to the situation. Assume that it is \$6,894.16. Then we compute the profit thus:—

Mdse. on hand Jan. 1		\$5,643.75
Bought January	\$2,644.18	
" February	1,845.17	
" March	1,929.44	
Total bought		6,418.79
		12,062.54
Total cost		
But there remains *unsold* at cost		6,894.16
Therefore the goods sold must have cost		5,168.38
But they produced		
In January	\$3,219.74	
February	2,454.62	
March	1,728.96—	7,403.32
and the profit must be		\$2,234.94

We can now complete our account (Fig.30).

FIG. 31
Merchandise

Jan. 1 Balance (Inventory)	\$5,643.75			
Jan. Purchases	2,644.18	Jan.	Sales	\$3,219.74
Feb. "	1,845.17	Feb.	"	2,454.62
March "	1,929.44	March	"	1,728.96
Profit	2,234.94		*Balance* (*Inventory*)	6,894.16
	\$14,297.48			\$14,297.48

\$6,894.16 goes to the balance-sheet; \$2,234.94 to the Profit and Loss Account.

This is the traditional form of the Merchandise Account, and suffices perfectly for "balancing the books." It nowhere presents, however, a clearly contrasted statement of the same goods at the two prices—in and out—and consequently the average percentage of profit could not be obtained without some effort.

When there are goods returned, whether purchases returned by us or sales returned to us, the confusion is still greater, for each side contains some values at cost price and some at selling price. To illustrate this, let us vary the above figures slightly, the final result being the same:—

Balance Jan. 1, as per inventory	\$5,643.75
Purchases January	2,760.18
of which returned	116.00
Sales January	3,452.74
of which returned	233.00
Purchases February	1,865.17
of which returned	20.00
Sales February	2,937.62
of which returned	483.00
Purchases March	1,947.44
of which returned	18.00
Sales March	1,903.96
of which returned	175.00
Balance March 31, as per inventory,	

FIG. 32
Merchandise

Jan. 1	Balance	\$5,643.75			
"	Purchases	2,760.18	Jan.	Returns	\$116.00
"	Returns	233.00	"	Sales	3,452.74
Feb.	Purchases	1,865.17	Feb.	Returns	20.00
"	Returns	483.00	"	Sales	2,937.62
March	Purchases	1,947.44	March	Returns	18.00
"	Returns	175.00	"	Sales	1,903.96
" 31	*Profit*	2,234.94	" 31	*Balance*	6,894.16
		\$15,342.48			\$15,342.48

It will be readily seen that the difficulty of obtaining intelligible information as to the comparative prices, in and out, is even greater than in Fig. 31, and that to obtain such information the account would need to be taken to pieces and made over. Now an account which needs to be made over is one that should have been made differently at first.

As an improvement, let us have three accounts instead of one—Purchases, Sales and Merchandise:—

FIG. 33
Merchandise

Jan. 1	Balance	\$5,643.75

Purchases

Jan. T'l purchased	\$2,760.18	Jan.	Returns	\$116.00
Feb. "	1,865.17	Feb.	"	20.00
March "	1,947.44	March	"	18.00

Sales

Jan. Returns	\$233.00	Jan.	Total sold	\$3,452.74
Feb. "	483.00	Feb.	"	2,937.62
March "	175.00	March	"	1,903.96

Next, close "Purchases" into Merchandise.

Purchases

Jan. T'l purchased	\$2,760.18	Jan.	Returns	\$116.00
Feb. "	1,865.17	Feb.	"	20.00
March "	1,947.44	March	"	18.00
			Net purchases	6,418.79
	\$6,572.79			\$6,572.79

Merchandise

Jan. 1	Balance	\$5,643.75
Jan.-Mar.	Purchases	6,418.79

Bring down the balance of Sales:—

Sales

Jan. Returns	\$233.00	Jan.	Total sales	\$3,452.74
Feb. "	483.00	Feb.	" "	2,937.62
March "	175.00	March	" "	1,903.96
Carried down	7,403.32			
	\$8,294.32			\$8,294.32
			Net proceeds	\$7,403.32

The two open accounts are Merchandise and Sales. Credit the former and debit the latter with the cost of the goods sold, computed as already shown; then both are ready to be transferred, the former to the balance-sheet, the latter to the Profit and Loss Account.

Merchandise

Jan. 1	Balance	$5,643.75			
Jan.-Mar.	Purchases	6,418.79	Jan.-Mar.	Cost of goods sold	$5,168.38
			Mar. 31	Balance	6,894.16
		$12,062.54			$12,062.54

Sales

Cost of goods sold	$5,168.38	Net proceeds	$7,403.32
Profit and Loss	2,234.94		
	$7,403.32		$7,403.32

The Purchase Account is not indispensable; but the Sales Account is specially recommended as disentangling the specific and the economic views of merchandise.

The General Principles of the Science of Accounts*

A Course of Lectures delivered before the School of Commerce, Accounts and Finance, New York University, 1900-1901, by Col. Charles E. Sprague, A. M., Ph.D., C.P.A., President of the Union Dime Savings Institution.

Revised for Commerce, Accounts and Finance.

IX.—SOURCES OF THE LEDGER.

Hitherto we have recognized no book except the ledger, which is really *the* book of account. All others are either transcripts from it or are conveniences for forming the ledger. The latter class has latterly been spoken of as *Posting Mediums*, a term introduced, I believe, by Mr. Hall, an English accountant.

In most of the works on bookkeeping "books of original entry" are treated of; but it is a fact that nowadays hardly any original entries are made in books. In modern business the primary record of transactions is made chiefly on documents, separate papers. Frequently those come to be books. As Mr. Kittredge has well said, we make up our books nowadays by manufacturing the leaves and afterwards binding them together. We used to think that we had to bind up the book first and then do the writing in it. But a blank book isn't at all necessary in modern business for the recording of transactions. Consider in how many ways in modern business a voucher is used, even down to the paying for fare on the elevated railroad. Hardly any business is done strictly by word of mouth without some documentary record, and it is entirely practicable to use such documents as posting mediums. What used to be called journalizing, ascertaining debits and credits, is now done by merely having different blanks printed. If you once establish the fact that a sale of merchandise on credit means a debit to some person's account and a credit to merchandise, if you print that on the blanks (though hardly necessary), and then record the amount and the name and the specification of the merchandise and the date, that is just as good an

entry of the transaction as it would be if written in the sales book.

THE DAY BOOK AND JOURNAL.

In works on bookkeeping we are generally informed that the book of original entry is the day book. This was true many years ago, but it is not true at the present day. This day book was supposed to contain a non-technical narrative of each transaction as it occurred. I have never seen such a book in actual use, nor heard any one claim to have seen it. It is a kind of myth or tradition.

The contents of the day book were to be transcribed into the journal in such form as to set forth the debits and the credits arising from each transaction and the amount of each. In other words, the narrative of the day book was rewritten in the form of *entries*, which have already been illustrated.

Compound entries—that is, those containing more than one debit or more than one credit—usually contained the term "sundries," a word rather ornamental than useful. Thus, if Cash were debit and Bills Receivable and Interest both credited, the entry was not simply

Cash Dr.	$........	
To Bills Receivable		$........
" Interest		$........

but,

Cash Dr. to Sundries	$........	
To Bills Receivable		$........
" Interest		$........

Similarly, several debtors to one creditor would be headed

Sundries Dr. to ....

If there were two or more items on each side, then the formula was

Sundries	Dr. to Sundries
Cash	Dr.
Merchandise "	
	To Bills Receivable
	" Interest

This form of the journal lingers still in partial use, but as a re-statement of each fact in a day book it is entirely obsolete.

POSTING MEDIUMS.

The journal is the original posting medium, and the method of posting the ledger from it remains unchanged even in its modified forms. Each line in the journal becomes an item in the ledger; if a debit, the corresponding credit is entered in the ledger, thus. "To ....," or, if there are several, "To Sundries;" on the credit side are entered "By ....," or "By Sundries."

The page of the journal is entered in the ledger and the page of the ledger in the journal, for reference either way.

EVOLUTION OF THE JOURNAL.

The journal being the simplest type of posting medium, we may treat the more elaborate forms historically as gradual modifications of the type.

The first step was to substitute for the single day book a series of specialized day books, each containing a certain kind of entry. Thus the Sales Book was a day book, containing only entries of the form ".......... Dr. to Mdse.;" the Purchase Book (more frequently, but less appositely, called Invoice Book), a collection of the form "Mdse. Dr. to ......;" while the Cash Book, on its two sides, followed the formulas "Cash Dr. to ...." and "........ Dr. to Cash." Such books are generally known as Auxiliary Books.

MONTHLY JOURNALIZING.

Now a great simplification in the journal became possible. Here was the bulk of the transactions already partly assorted, or, as it might be expressed, half journalized. Instead of transcribing each sale, or purchase, or receipt, or payment, into the journal, one grand entry could be made for each class, covering a length of time, usually a month; hence this process of wholesale journalizing is usually termed "monthly journalizing."

If the books used are the ones mentioned above, four entries would be necessary; for the sales

    Sundries Dr. to Mdse.
    John Smith
    William Jones
        &c.

For the purchases

    Mdse. Dr. to Sundries
        To Acker & Merrill
        " Park & Tilford
            &c.

For the receipts,

    Cash Dr. to Sundries
        &c.

For the payments,

    Sundries Dr. to Cash
        &c.

Evidently this process would save nearly half the writing in the journal, and, besides, would have the advantage of generalizing the cash and merchandise accounts and making their entries more symmetrical. In almost any kind of business the mass of the transactions would thus be disposed of, but there would be a residuum of mixed character which would require special journalization; this, however, would usually be made direct without the preliminary of a day book.

But while much time is thus saved in journalizing, nothing can be posted till the end of the month. The journal blocks the way—everything must wait for it. Hence it will be well towards the end of the month before the trial balance of the preceding month can be completed. A remedy must be found for this.

each a transaction; why not use these same documents for making up the ledger? In a sale, for example, the document will be a bill of goods. Instead of entering the bill in the Sales Book and then copying its amount into the ledger, turn at once to the ledger page with the bill in the hand, post the amount, and in some way note on the bill the fact that it has been posted.

The advantages of posting directly from the document are the following:—

1. The eye is close to the figures to be posted and the place where the posting is to be; the eye does not have to carry its memory of the figures across the pages of two big books.

2. There is no other amount above or below to be confused with the one in question.

3. The documents may first be assorted in such order that only one passage through the ledger will be necessary, not skipping backward and forward.

Posting from documents saves time and prevents errors.

PHYSICAL POSTING.

We have arrived at the point where a document makes the circuit of the counting-room as an embodiment of a transaction, leaving its impress in each place where it is required. Suppose the document is an invoice representing a purchase. After going the rounds it must be preserved. Then, instead of copying it into an invoice book or purchase book, the device is adopted of pasting it into a scrap-book. If this book has a money column, it becomes a real purchase book, and the labor of copying the invoices is entirely eliminated.

Invoices outward, or bills for sales, are treated in an analogous way, the original being press-copied or a typewritten carbon copy being pasted in, making up a sales book on the lines of the purchase scrap-book. Or, very recently, the book typewriter has enabled this to be done more neatly still. The bill is made out in typewriting, and the book record is made simultaneously, one being the original and the other the carbon copy.

Another mechanical development is the combined listing and adding machine of various types which furnishes a detailed statement in duplicate for both parties, and also a total.

We are only in the infancy of what I have called "physical" bookkeeping, the mechanical, chemical or photographic multiplication of data, instead of copying and re-copying.

It will be noticed that these devices are most easily applicable to what may be called the "staple" books, books like the sales book and purchase book, which contain only transactions of one form, and that one a simple, not a complex entry.

Where the business is not such as to give rise to these long series of straightforward entries, but present a more various and mixed character, another method is requisite in order to condense the postings, and this we will next consider.

The General Principles of the Science of Accounts*

A Course of Lectures delivered before the School of Commerce, Accounts and Finance, New York University, 1900-1901, by Col. Charles E. Sprague, A. M., Ph.D., C.P.A., President of the Union Dime Savings Institution.

Revised for Commerce, Accounts and Finance.

DIRECT POSTING.

Taking the Sales Book as a type, it must be evident that the posting would be just as accurate if the amount of the sale were posted thence direct to the debit of the purchaser as if it first passed through the ceremonial of the journal. By adding a "folio column" to the Sales Book, the thing is accomplished: the Sales Book becomes a posting medium. At the end of the month it is again observed that the total to be credited to merchandise account may as well be made up here as in the journal and posted accordingly. When this is done in all the auxiliary books, we have rendered the journal useless. These books, no longer auxiliaries, but principals, are themselves specialized journals. The journal is required only for the exceptional entries.

In the Cash Book it may be noted that we have a complete Cash Account; why, then, not dispense with the Cash Account in the ledger? Consider the Cash Book as *being* the Cash Account, simply kept for convenience in a second volume. When an "original entry" has been made in this book, it is already half posted; the other half of the posting consists in carrying the same amount to the *reverse* side of some other account.

Thus we have the results of the journal short-circuited; there is an almost complete saving of the labor which was expended in keeping the journal in the manner previously described.

DOCUMENT POSTING.

These direct posting books were doubtless made up from vouchers or other documents representing

The General Principles of the Science of Accounts*

A Course of Lectures delivered before the School of Commerce, Accounts and Finance, New York University, 1900-1901, by Col. Charles E. Sprague, A. M., Ph.D., C.P.A., President of the Union Dime Savings Institution.

Revised for Commerce, Accounts and Finance.

XI.—COLUMNAR POSTING MEDIUMS.

Starting again with the simple journal, and discarding the day book, we will trace the evolution of another quite different mechanism for the convenient distribution of items to the accounts to which they relate. In the former development we introduced separate and specialized *books;* now we introduce separate and specialized *columns.*

Looking through the pages of any journal it will be seen that a few accounts appear in the majority of the items. If, then, we have extra columns ruled for these and insert in the regular column only other items than these, we can defer posting such frequent

accounts until the end of the month or as long as we please.

For such columnar journals, the form where the money columns are on the outside and the wording in the middle, is often the most convenient. Thus, if it is found that in the regular run of the business a large number of the debit items are to go to Cash, Merchandise and Expense, and a large proportion of the credits are to Cash, Merchandise and Interest, then four columns on each side would be necessary, or eight in all.

The word "Sundries" is here used to designate all other accounts than Cash, Merchandise, Interest and Expense. Amounts in the "Sundries" column are separately posted to the appropriate accounts, and in order to trace them a folio column is ruled next the sundries column.

At the bottom of each page a footing of all the columns should be made and the totals carried to the head of the next page. The sum of the debits will, if correct, be equal to the sum of the credits. The total of the special columns will be posted in a lump at the end of the month or other period, thus saving a great deal of writing and turning of leaves.

Besides this economy of time and space, the columnar method is useful for keeping group accounts

Dr.				Fig. 35.—Columnar Journal.		Cr.		
Expense	Mdse.	Cash	Sundries	Entry	Sundries	Cash	Mdse.	Interest

and subordinate accounts without using two grades of ledger. Thus, in discussing James Jones' Balance Sheet (Fig. 17), we found the item, "Due from various personal debtors, $15,972.18." We explained that this was the aggregate of a number of individual accounts. By adding to the columnar journal two more special columns, "Accounts Receivable, Dr.," and "Accounts Receivable, Cr.," we may at any time ascertain the aggregate by balancing these two columns; but we must also post the items to the individual accounts, for which purpose another folio column should be left on each side.

Any number of aggregate accounts or group accounts may thus be kept, obviating the necessity of a general ledger with subordinates.

It is not necessary here to give more than a glance at the principle of columnization, but it may be carried to any extent, and is often overdone. Too many columns defeat their purpose.

Not only may the journal be columnized, but also the specialized posting mediums, already described, and especially is this true of the cash book, which readily lends itself to this treatment. When almost all the normal entries are in cash (as in banking) the journal is often dispensed with, and the special columns of the cash book, *in pairs*, made to do journal duty.

There is great waste of paper in a book of very many columns. But it is not absolutely necessary to have each amount exactly in line with its descriptive entry. Let the right hand page be divided into little spaces and the left hand page be a two-column journal. Then go through, picking out all the debits to some one account, and then to another, until all the items have been distributed into these little spaces, which are then added and proved as well as, even better than, if they were columns running from top to bottom. This plan has been called SIDE POSTING.

CROSS TOTALS.

If a columnar book of any kind has a total column in which is entered the amount of every line, there will result a double proof by vertical and lateral addition.

For example, let us set down sixteen numbers in four lines (1, 2, 3, 4) and in four columns (a, b, c, d).

	1.	2.	3.	4.
a...........	129	233	532	279
b...........	817	365	200	474
c...........	516	799	344	672
d...........	625	375	992	101
	...	...	...	...

Let us set the total of each column at the bottom and the total of each line at the beginning, as indicated by the dots.

FIG. 36.

	Total	1	2	3	4
a	1173	129	233	532	279
b	1856	817	365	200	474
c	2331	516	799	344	672
d	2093	625	375	992	101
Total	7453	2087	1772	2068	1526

The grand total, 7,453, is not only the sum of the line totals (1,713 + 1,856 + 2,331 + 2,093), but it is the sum of the column totals (2,087 + 1,772 + 2,068 + 1,526). This is the tabular form of account or statement. We introduce it here because there is a decided advantage in reducing a columnar book to the tabular form, and thus making it self-proving.

To take a column of amounts like these,

		1	2	3	4
a	1173				
b	1856				
c	2331				
d	2093				
	7453				

and analyzing each amount into its components, fill the columns 1, 2, 3, 4, so as to produce the result shown in Fig. 36, is usually called *distributing;* the French and Italian authors, however, are now in the habit of calling it *developing* or *unrolling,* as if the single column at the left were a paper folded or rolled, showing only the totals, which is unfolded or unrolled, making a tabular statement. This unrolling constitutes the principal process in the system known as *logismography.* Instead of building up the general accounts by combining the minor accounts, it begins with the most general statement, usually in two accounts only, one representing ASSETS AND LIABILITIES, the other PROPRIETORSHIP. This pair of accounts constitutes what is called the Logismographic Journal. Each of the two accounts is "unrolled" into a "First Development"; each column of this is again developed, and so on to any degree of subdivision.

The General Principles of the Science of Accounts*

A Course of Lectures delivered before the School of Commerce, Accounts and Finance, New York University, 1900-1901, by Col. Charles E. Sprague, A. M., Ph.D., C.P.A., President of the Union Dime Savings Institution.

Revised for Commerce, Accounts and Finance.

XII.—ANNULLING OR OFFSETTING ACCOUNTS.

While normally all debit balances are assets and all credit balances are either liabilities or proprietorship, yet under some special circumstances accounts are maintained for the purpose of diminishing, annulling or offsetting some balance of the opposite side.

A credit balance, instead of being a payable or proprietary item, may represent merely the extinction of some asset. Thus, having receivables of the aggregate amount of $10,000, we may perhaps anticipate that some loss will probably be experienced before this is all collected; we may estimate that $500 will thus prove uncollectable and that the actual value of the receivables is therefore $9,500. It is, however, essential to keep the account of each debtor correctly stated regardless of any assumed shrinkage; we cannot tell upon which accounts the shrinkage will fall. We therefore keep open an account which is an assumed deduction or extinction of so much of the value of the receivables, entitling it "Reserve against bad debts" or something analogous.

Again, it may be desirable to keep a permanent account of the original cost of some asset which is progressively depreciating, representing such depreciation by a credit account, which is not liability, nor is it proprietorship. Securities bought at a premium, which must disappear at maturity, are frequently treated in this manner. The main account is retained at the original cost, while such part of the premium as vanishes during each period, instead of being de-

ducted, is credited to an "Amortisation" account. Here is a credit balance, which is an offset to an asset.

Similarly there may be debit balances, at first sight appearing to be assets, but in reality offsets to liabilities or proprietorship. "Treasury Stock," or "Un-issued Shares," is an offset to Capital Stock, and not an asset at all. Another instance of offset against capital has been already given in Fig. 22.

In all cases of offset the two opposing balances may be at any time combined and their difference used as a net resultant. In making up an analytical statement from a balance sheet, it is recommended that the difference alone appear in the column, the deduction being made previously. Thus, instead of the two opposing balances:

Personal Accounts Receivable.	$10,000	Reserve against Bad Debts,	$500

let it read thus:

Personal Accounts Receivable,	$10,000	
less Reserve against Bad Debts,	500	
	$9,500	

THEORIES OF DEBIT AND CREDIT.

In my explanations of principles, I have treated the system of accounts mathematically or quantitatively, as an equation of values expressed in terms of money. We have ascertained the components of each side of the equation, and those components were by no means all of the same kind. But to some minds the facts of accounts present themselves more as relations than as quantities, and to those a more satisfying theory than the mathematical one is one where all debits are classed as one kind of relations, and all credits, if possible, as one other kind.

Thus, there are different theories of accounts extant, and various authors have advocated them. All are consonant with truth or are different ways of looking at truth. And so far as numerical results are concerned, they all come to the same thing. They are rather different ways of naming results and processes than differences in the things themselves.

It is well to keep the mind open and to be ready to

use, rather than combat, any of these theories. In discussing any question of accounts, you can make better progress by looking at it from the point of view of him who is consulting with you, rather than by compelling him to come over to your ground.

Taking up first the debit side of the balance sheet, our point of view has been that assets were of two kinds: 1. Things in possession, or property; 2. Claims against others, debts due us, or, as we will now say for brevity, *receivables*.

The following are among the variant theories as to debits:—

1. ALL ASSETS TREATED AS RECEIVABLES.—Doubtless the earliest bookkeeping was of receivables only. Property spoke for itself; it was right there, a concrete entity, needing no account. When the need arose for keeping account of money also, the box, "Cassa," was personified as owing so much to the owner. Following this line of thought all property in possession came to be treated as due or receivable.

There is a large number of categories, ordinarily thought of as property, which logically are only receivables. Take cash itself. In an ordinary business house the vastly greater part of the cash is in the bank, and the bank is certainly a mere debtor for the amount. If there is also cash on hand, it will usually be for the most part in notes; bank-notes or notes of the nation. These are not literally property, but receivables; representatives of value to be had on demand. Thus, only a small fraction of the cash, namely, the coin, is property in a literal sense. Nay, some might contend that, as the subsidiary coin was only a token, it too was but a representative of a claim; and, if there happened to be no gold coin in the drawer, a large cash balance would consist entirely of receivables.

Bonds payable to bearer and carrying interest-coupons might at first sight seem to be property, but strictly are evidence of debt.

It is thus seen that without any strain a great part of the assets may be legitimately classed as mere receivables, and in the theory which I have followed in these lectures it would be a matter of indifference whether they be treated as property or as receivables; that question may be left entirely in abeyance in the quantitative theory; the values are assets, think of them as you please; they are positives or actives in the balance sheet.

But if it is deemed desirable to reduce everything, for uniformity's sake, to receivables, a little artifice is necessary. This is employed in two different ways.

a. THE COST METHOD.—This piece of property owes me so much, because I have put so much into it, just as this man owes me so much because I have put so much into his hands. In this way property is recognized as existing; but the standard of debit is how much other property I parted with or promised for it.

b. THE AGENCY METHOD.—My cash is entirely in charge of a cashier; let us consider that he owes me the amount. I need not pay any attention to whether it is in bank, in paper, or in coin; it is a receivable from Mr. Cashier. I may ask him to exhibit it for inspection as often as I like, for he is only my agent, and he must obey my instructions in disposing of it; but otherwise it is a debt. . . . I appoint another agent to take charge of my merchandise, and when I debit Merchandise I mean that Mr. Storekeeper is charged with that value, for which he must account

to me, having administered his trust according to my rules. . . . My real estate agent is my debtor for the property placed in his hands. Thus I appoint agents or heads of all my departments and keep an account with each. In this way all assets are reduced to receivables, and property as such is eliminated from the accounts.

If I conduct some parts of my business in person, I may consider myself as my own agent in that respect, dividing my functions as proprietor and as manager.

Continental writers on accounts often style these agents *consignataries*, and the actual, outside, debtors and creditors as *correspondents*, and they use the word *agency* to designate the whole body of consignataries and correspondents, or the whole array of the balance sheet outside of the proprietor.

2. ALL ASSETS TREATED AS PROPERTY.—This view is diametrically opposed to the former, yet it too has a basis of truth. Is not property in the background of all receivables? Although we cannot touch it directly, we can ultimately; it may not be "spot" property, but the tangible value exists and is the reason of our trusting. We own a portion of the property of each debtor; we can ultimately, by process of law, seize enough to satisfy the claim. It is like owning a half-interest in a house or a horse; we cannot take away a physical half, yet no one would deny that the half-interest is property, if anything is.

This is sometimes called the *materialistic* view as distinguished from the *personalistic*; and the quantitative view which we used is called the *mixed*, because it recognizes both the personal and the material aspect, both the relational and the existential.

Now as to the credit side.

3. ALL CREDITS TREATED AS LIABILITIES OR PAYABLES.—This view makes proprietorship a liability. The question then arises, a liability to whom? Who owes him? The answer is twofold.

a. If all assets are receivables (Theory 1), then the balance sheet is a complex statement of indebtedness, and the debtors on the left side jointly owe the creditors (including proprietors) on the right. Some debtors, such as the cashier, are more readily to be reached than others; some creditors, on the other hand, are entitled to priority, the proprietors being the last of the liabilities to be liquidated, in consideration of participation in profits. Or,

b. An intermediate entity, *the business*, owes the full amount of the balance sheet (on the grounds of Theory 1, a) to the outside creditors and to the proprietor; on the other hand, this same aggregate is owed by the debtors (including property either by the "cost" or the "agency" view) to the business. "The business" is always in equilibrium; it cannot be owed without simultaneously owing the corresponding value. Thus, the capitalist, so far as this particular business is concerned, is a creditor for the amount invested. His own proprietary books would show him as creditor for various investments and finally the balance sheet would show his net worth, if any.

A trustee account, where all values are handled for the benefit of some one else, is the purest instance of this view. Such a trust is exemplified in the savings bank, meaning the purely mutual savings bank organized, for example, under the New York law. In this, the bank, legally speaking, is the board of trustees; they hold all the assets, but entirely for the benefit of the depositors, to whom they owe (assuming there are no other creditors) every cent's worth of the assets; for the surplus has been legally decided to be joint deposits. Here the neutral intermediary exists in fact, not merely in imagination; the creditor for all the debts and debtor for all the credits.

Continental writers who adopt this view usually speak of the *administrator* or *manager* as the intermediary between debtors and creditors.

It is to be noted that even when payables and proprietorships are classed together as liabilities, care is usually taken to distinguish them as "outside" and "inside liabilities" or as "non-participating" and "participating liabilities." As long as this line is drawn it does not so much matter in what words the credits are described. And it must be observed that while the outside liabilities are rigid, the inside liabilities are elastic and vary with every expansion or contraction of the values of the assets.

4. ALL CREDITS TREATED AS PROPRIETORSHIP.— Here is an array of assets; who owns them? They equitably belong to the payables as much as to the proprietors; the latter take precedence as to management, but the former in case of distribution.

The results of this phase are very similar to those of 3. In both, payables and proprietorship are regarded as different degrees of the same kind of tenure,—not, as I have placed it before you, as different and in fact contrasting tenures.

5. PAYABLES TREATED AS NEGATIVE ASSETS, PROPRIETORSHIP AS NET ASSETS.—This is the extreme mathematical view and was advanced by Joseph Hardcastle. It reduces the entire system to a collection of assets, stated twofold. It requires sufficient algebraic training to be able to conceive of negative quantities dissociated from positives, but when this is attained it gives perfectly clear demonstration of all the processes. It is consistent with either view of the debit side, the personal, the material or the mixed. It makes the line of cleavage not down the center between debits and credits, but as in our Fig. 27, between specific and economic accounts.

Instead of combating these various points of view, I recommend that you utilize them to broaden your comprehension. Apply them in succession to any set of accounts or any balance sheet and observe what modification in statement is necessary to make it conform to the various terms of the personalistic, the materialistic or the quantitative theories.

THE END.

The Accountancy of Investment

Studies in Business

First Series, No. 3

THE ACCOUNTANCY OF INVESTMENT

INCLUDING A TREATISE ON COMPOUND INTEREST, ANNUITIES, AMORTISATION, AND THE VALUATION OF SECURITIES

BY CHARLES EZRA SPRAGUE, A.M., PH.D., C.P.A., PROFESSOR IN THE NEW YORK UNIVERSITY SCHOOL OF COMMERCE, ACCOUNTS AND FINANCE; PRESIDENT OF THE UNION DIME SAVINGS INSTITUTION; CHAIRMAN OF THE SAVINGS BANK SECTION OF THE AMERICAN BANKERS ASSOCIATION : : :

PUBLISHED FOR THE NEW YORK UNIVERSITY SCHOOL OF COMMERCE, ACCOUNTS AND FINANCE BY THE BUSINESS PUBLISHING COMPANY NEW YORK, 1904

TRUNK BROS.
96 WILLIAM STREET
NEW YORK

PREFACE.

The following chapters embrace the substance of lectures delivered before the classes of the NEW YORK UNIVERSITY SCHOOL OF COMMERCE, ACCOUNTS AND FINANCE. They have been in many places condensed, and in others expanded, with a view to their use as a text-book.

I have introduced a treatise on Interest, Discount, Annuities, Sinking Funds, Amortisation and Valuation of Bonds, as I had not been able to find any suitable text-book which I could recommend. I hope that this will be useful to many who desire to inaugurate more scientific methods in their accountancy, but are unable to find intelligible rules for the computations. Treatises on the subject written for actuarial students are invariably too difficult, except for those who have not only been highly trained in algebra, but are fresh in its use, and this makes the subject forbidding to many minds. I have made all my demonstrations arithmetical and illustrative, but, I think, none the less convincing and intelligible.

I am indebted to Prof. Joseph Hardcastle, C.P.A., and to Walter E. Hallett, A.B., for valuable suggestions and assistance.

CHARLES E. SPRAGUE.

New York, November, 1904.

TABLE OF CONTENTS.

INTRODUCTORY CHAPTER.

THE THEORY OF ACCOUNTS.

CHAPTER I.

CAPITAL AND REVENUE.

CHAPTER II.

INTEREST.

CHAPTER III.

THE USE OF LOGARITHMS.

CHAPTER IV.

AMOUNT OF AN ANNUITY.

CHAPTER V.

PRESENT WORTH OF AN ANNUITY.

CHAPTER VI.

Rent of Annuity and Sinking Fund.

CHAPTER VII.

Nominal and Effective Rates.

CHAPTER VIII.

Valuation of Bonds.

CHAPTER IX.

Forms of Account—General Principles.

CHAPTER X.

REAL ESTATE MORTGAGES.

CHAPTER XI.

LOANS ON COLLATERAL.

CHAPTER XII.

INTEREST ACCOUNTS.

CHAPTER XIII.

BONDS AND SIMILAR SECURITIES.

CHAPTER XIV.

DISCOUNTED VALUES.

APPENDIX I.

APPENDIX II.

APPENDIX III.

THE ACCOUNTANCY OF INVESTMENT.

FIRST EDITION.

[Readers are requested to mark these errata in their copies, or to refer to them in the margin.]

Page 19, Article 22.—*For* .88487 *read* .888487, *in two places.*

Page 31, Article 69, 4th line from end.—*Comma after* annually, *not after* aside.

Page 32, 3d line from bottom.—*For* decrease, *read* increase.

Page 37, Article 92.—*7th and 8th lines should read:* Hence .2349502 is the present value of $1 at 3% per period for 49 periods. *Etc.*

Page 38, last line.—*Decimal point omitted in* 4,491.29.

Page 39.—*Strike out the number* 94 —*This should not be a new paragraph, but part of the preceding.*

Page 47, Schedule I.—*In the heading, for* Net come *read* Net Income.

Page 50, 3d line from bottom.—*For* $4\frac{8}{10}$ *read* $4\frac{1}{8}$.

Page 70, Article 157, 1st line.—*For* 149, *read* 146.

Page 75.—*Add this footnote to Article 168.*
——*Bonds purchased *flat* should be separated into principal and interest.

Page 89, Article 193.—*This should read* 194, *and the succeeding articles should be renumbered to the last, which is* 198.

THE ACCOUNTANCY OF INVESTMENT.

INTRODUCTORY CHAPTER.

THEORY OF ACCOUNTS.

The **Balance Sheet** of a business expresses the status of that business at a certain point of time. It normally contains three classes of values: assets, liabilities and proprietorship, and expresses an equation between *one* of these classes, the assets, and the *two* others. As a fact, stripped of all technicality, the assets are always exactly equal to the sum of the liabilities and the proprietorship:

$$\text{Assets} = \text{Liabilities} + \text{Proprietorship}.$$

This is merely an inverted way of defining proprietorship as being the excess of assets over liabilities:

$$\text{Assets} - \text{Liabilities} = \text{Proprietorship}.$$

In practice we generally write the equation in the form of a ledger account:

ASSETS :	LIABILITIES :
. . . . $	. . . . $
. . . .	. . . .
. . . .	. . . .
. . . .	Proprietorship
. . . .	. . . .
. . . .	. . . .
[Equal Totals]	

As the proprietorship is simply the excess of assets over liabilities, it is evident that at any moment, *if the facts are all ascertained*, the same equation must hold good; it must be perpetually true that, through all shiftings and changes:

$$\text{Assets} = \text{Liabilities} + \text{Proprietorship}.$$

This is the equation of accountancy, and all the processes of bookkeeping depend upon it.

The following is a condensed balance sheet of the affairs of an individual in business:

BALANCE SHEET OF WILLIAM SMITH.

Cash	$5,082.34	Bills Payable	$8,000.00
Merchandise	17,082.65	Personal Creditors	5,465.35
Personal Debtors	8,123.17		
Bills Receivable	7,000.00	*William Smith*	*23,822.81*
	$37,288.16		$37,288.16

The assets are partly composed of property, actually in possession, and partly of debts due to Smith; while the liabilities are entirely indebtedness due *by* Smith.

The net proprietorship is designated by the name of the proprietor, although this is not universally the case.

Instead of a single proprietor there may be a partnership, and the proprietorship may be represented either separately or in aggregate, as follows:

BALANCE SHEET OF JONES & SMITH.

Cash	$8,589.09	Bills Payable	$8,000.00
Merchandise	39,249.38	Personal Creditors	5,465.35
Bills Receivable	7,000.00	Mortgage Payable	4,000.00
Personal Debtors	24,095.32	*James Jones*	*47,645.63*
Real Estate	10,000.00	*William Smith*	*23,822 81*
	$88,933.79		$88,933.79

BALANCE SHEET OF JONES & SMITH.

Cash	$8,589.09	Bills Payable	$8,000.00
Merchandise	39,249.38	Personal Creditors	5,465.35
Bills Receivable	7,000.00	Mortgage Payable	4,000.00
Personal Debtors	24,095.32	*Jones & Smith* *(their joint capital)*	*71,468 44*
Real Estate	10,000.00		
	$88,933.79		$88,933.79

Let it be supposed that Messrs. Jones & Smith, instead of a partnership, had preferred to form a company, named the Jones Mercantile Company. They consider that, as the actual value of their joint proprietorship is over $71,000, it would be quite proper to capitalize it at $60,000, in 600 shares, of $100 each. Nevertheless, there is a total proprietorship of $71,468.44, as before, all of which must be represented in some form.

In order to represent both the amount of the capitalization and the true proprietary value, we divide the total proprietorship into two parts : —

Capital : par, or face value of shares	$60,000.00
Surplus : excess of real value over par	11,468.44
Their sum is the real proprietorship	$71,468.44

The resulting balance sheet would be : —

BALANCE SHEET OF THE JONES MERCANTILE COMPANY.

Cash	$8,589.09	Bills Payable	$8,000.00
Merchandise	39,249.38	Personal Creditors	5,465.35
Bills Receivable	7,000.00	Mortgage Payable	4,000.00
Personal Debtors	24,095.32	*Capital Stock*	*60,000.00*
Real Estate	10,000.00	*Surplus*	*11,468.44*
	$88,933.79		$88,933.79

These are the usual forms of the balance sheet. As our debtors are all on the left hand side, and our creditors are on the right, it has become customary to call the left the *debit* side, and the right, the *credit* side, notwithstanding the debit side contains much more than debtors and the creditor side much more than creditors.

A better term for the debit side of the balance sheet is the Active ; and for the credit side, the **Passive.**

The Passive has two widely different sets of values : the liabilities and the proprietorship, and I see no advantage in stretching the term " liabilities " to cover both. To call the proprietorship a liability is purely a technicality ; the part owned is precisely that part which is *free* from liability.

The balance sheet presents the status at some certain point of time.   We need also some means for recording what occurs, for the changes which take place between the balance sheets. For this purpose, the ledger is opened, being a system of accounts ; one account at least for each line of the balance sheet. It was formerly supposed that these accounts must be kept in one invariable form, regardless of their nature, such form being substantially that of the balance sheets shown above. Although this is no longer the rule we will employ the traditional form in this illustration.

A miniature ledger made up from the balance sheet of the Jones Mercantile Company would begin somewhat after this fashion:

CASH.

Balance	$8,589.09		

BILLS PAYABLE.

		Balance	$8,000.00

MERCHANDISE.

Balance	$39,249.38		

BILLS RECEIVABLE.

Balance	$7,000.00		

"Personal Debtors" would probably comprise a number of accounts, headed by the name of each debtor.

Dr.	A. B.	Cr.
Balance		

"Personal Creditors" would likewise comprise a number of separate accounts.

Dr.	M. N.	Cr.
	Balance	

REAL ESTATE.		
Balance	$10,000.00	

Dr.	MORTGAGE PAYABLE.	Cr.
	Balance	$4,000.00

CAPITAL STOCK.		
	Balance	$60,000.00

Surplus.

		Balance	$11,468.44

Thus the balance sheet has been dissected and accounts have been opened for each department of the business. A single account might have been opened for "Personal Debtors," but in that case it would have to be expanded into subordinate accounts, so as to give information as to each debtor. The same is true of " Personal Creditors," which is also a group account.

For good reasons the balance with which each account begins is placed on the *same side* as it occupied in the balance sheet. Any increase of that balance will also be entered on the same side, and any decrease on the other side.

Any possible transaction will increase the debit (left hand) side of the ledger, and its credit (right hand) side to exactly the same amount. Let us consider some of the possible cases:

1. If any asset is increased, we must either
    part with some other asset,
    or run into debt,
    or, (if neither of these is true,)
    our wealth is increased.

That is, an increase of assets is attended by a decrease of assets, or an increase of liability, or an increase of proprietorship, one or more of them.

2. If a liability is increased, we must either
    receive some asset,
    or pay off some other liability,
    or else we have lost.

Therefore, an increase of liability is attended by an increase of assets, by a decrease of liability, or a decrease of proprietorship.

As there are three elements in the accounts — assets, liabilities and proprietorship — and as each of these may be increased or decreased, there are six possible entries, at least two of which arise from every transaction, as follows :

DEBITS.	CREDITS.
Increase of Assets.	Decrease of Assets.
Decrease of Liabilities.	Increase of Liabilities.
Decrease of Proprietorship.	Increase of Proprietorship.

The increase and decrease of proprietorship is called Profit and Loss. As it is of the utmost importance to study the causes of Profit and Loss, certain subsidiary accounts are opened for the sole purpose of classifying profits and losses according to their sources. At the time of constructing the next balance sheet, these subsidiary accounts (Interest, Rent, Expenses, Sales, etc.) are transferred to a general Profit and Loss account, which presents an analysis of the conduct of the business for the period elapsed. This Profit and Loss account is in turn transferred to the permanent Proprietary Accounts.

The foregoing is a sketch of the general theory of Double Entry Bookkeeping. There are various ways of looking at the subject, but I think this the most direct and best suited to the present purpose. For some other purposes, such as what may be called *juridical* accounts, the respective rights and obligations of the parties are the basis, rather than the struggle to increase proprietorship. The equation for this purpose would be :

Charge = Discharge + Accountability.

In general the equation comprises not two, but three, terms:

Positives = Negatives + Resultant.

CHAPTER I.

CAPITAL AND REVENUE.

1.—Capital is that portion of wealth which is set aside for the production of additional wealth. The capital of a business, therefore, is the whole or a part of the assets of the business, and, of course, appears on the active or debit side of its balance sheet. This is the sense in which the word "capital" is used in economics; but in bookkeeping the words "capital account" are often used in quite another sense to mean accounts on the credit or passive side which denote proprietorship. To prevent confusion, I will avoid the use of this expression, capital account.

2.— Use of Capital. In active business capital must be employed — must be combined with skill and industry to produce more wealth. Businesses, and consequently their accounting methods, vary as to the manner in which capital is used. Cash is potential capital of all kinds, as desired. In a manufacturing business it is exchanged for machinery, appliances, raw materials, labor, which transforms the material into the product. In mercantile business it is expended for goods, bought at one price, to sell at another, and for collecting, displaying, caring for, advertising and delivering the goods. To bridge over the time between selling and collecting, additional capital is required, usually known as "working capital," but which might be more appropriately styled "waiting capital." Thus we may analyse each kind of business and show that its capital assets depend upon the character of the business.

3.—Sources of Capital. On the other side of the balance sheet the capital must be accounted for as to who furnishes it. Here there are two sharply divided classes: loan-capital or liability, and own capital or proprietorship. The great distinction is that the latter participates in the profits and bears the losses, while the former takes its share irrespective of the success of the concern. It is the own-capital which is referred to in the phrase "capital account."

4.—While we often speak of a man's capital as being *invested* in the business, yet when we use the word more strictly, we confine it to the non-participating sense. Thus we say, he not only owns the business, but he has some *investments* besides. In the strictest sense, then, *investment* implies divesting one's self of the possession and control of one's assets and granting such possession and control to another. The advantage of the use of the capital must be great enough to enable the user to earn more than the sum which he pays to the investor or capitalist. There are many cases where the surrender is not absolute, and there is more or less risk assumed by the investor. This I should call not absolute investment, but to some extent partnership. The essence of strict investment is vicarious earning, a share of the gain not dependent on the fortunes of the handler.

5.—Revenue. All investment is made with a view to revenue, which is the share of the earnings given for the use of capital. This takes three forms: interest, rent and dividends — the former two corresponding to strict investment, and the latter to participation.

6.—Interest and rent do not essentially differ. Both are stipulated payments for the use of capital; but in the latter the same physical asset must be returned on the completion of the contract. If you borrow a dollar, you may repay any dollar you please; if you hire a house or a horse, you may not return any house or any horse, but must produce the identical one you had. Interest and rent are both proportionate to time.

7.—Dividends. These are profits paid over to the owners of the own-capital, whether partners or shareholders. The amount is subtracted from the collective assets and paid over to the separate owners. Theoretically there is no profit nor loss in this distribution. I have more cash, but my share in the collective assets is exactly that much less. It is distributed, partly because it is needed by the participants for consumption; partly because no more capital can be profitably used in the enterprise. Some concerns, for example some banks, which can profitably use more capital, and whose shareholders do not require it for consumption, refrain from dividing, and the accumulation inures just as surely to the shareholders, and is realizable through increased value of the shares upon sale. Thus, dividends are not strictly revenue. Yet the shareholder may treat them as such ; the dividend may be so regular as practically to be fixed, or his shares may be preferential, so that to some extent he is receiving an ascertained amount ; or, as in case of a leased railway, it may be fixed by contract. Still, legally speaking, the dividend is instantaneous, and does not accrue, like interest and rent.

8.—As all investment is really the buying of revenue, and as the value of the investment depends largely upon the amount of revenue, and as the typical form of revenue is interest, it is, therefore, necessary to study the laws of interest, including those more complex forms—annuities, sinking funds and amortisation. Although there is a special branch of accountancy — the actuarial—which deals not only with these subjects, but with life and other contingencies, yet it is very necessary for the general accountant to understand at least the principles of the subject.

CHAPTER II.

INTEREST.

9.—The elements of interest are **rate, time** and **principal.**

10.—The **time** is divided into periods ; at the end of each period a certain sum for each unit of the principal is payable. The ratio between the unit of principal and the sum paid for its use is the **rate,** and is expressed in hundredths or "per centum." Thus, if the contract is to pay three cents for each dollar of principal each year, it may be expressed, .03 per annum, 3 per centum per annum, 3 per cent., or 3%. Where the period is not yearly, but a less time, it is customary to speak, nevertheless, of the annual rate. Thus, instead of 3% per half year, we say 6%, payable semi-annually. Instead of 1% per quarter, we say 4%, quarterly. In our discussions of interest, however, we shall treat of *periods* and of the rate per period, in order to avoid complication.

11.—As the law does not recognize interest for any fraction of a day, it becomes necessary to inquire what is meant by a half year or a quarter. The Statutory Construction Law (Chapter 677, Laws of 1892, § 25) solves this difficulty by prescribing that a half year is not 182½ days, but six calendar months, and that a quarter is not 91¼ days, but three calendar months.

Calendar months are computed as follows : — Commence at the day from which the reckoning is made, excluding that day ; then the day in the next month having the same number will at its close complete the first month ; the second month will end with the same numbered day, and so on to the same day of the final month. One difficulty arises : Suppose we have started with the 31st and the last month has only 30 days or less. Then, the law says, the month ends with the last day. One month from January 31st, 1904, was February 29th ; one month from January 30th or January 29th would also terminate on February 29th; in a common year, not a leap year, the last day would be February 28th.

12.—A **Day** also requires definition. The legal day begins and ends at midnight. In reckoning from one day to another you must not include the day *from which.* Thus, if a loan is made at any hour on the third of the month and paid at any hour on the fourth, there is one day's interest, and that one day is the fourth, not the third. Practically it is the nights that count. If five mid-nights have passed since the loan was made, then there is five days' interest accrued.

13.—**Parts of a period.** In practice any fraction of an interest period is computed at the corresponding fraction of the rate, although theoretically this is not quite just. If the regular period is a year, then the odd days should be reckoned as 365ths of a year. Also, if the contract is for days only and there is no mention of months, quarters or half years, then also a day is regarded as $\frac{1}{365}$ of a year. But when the contract is for months, quarters or half years, the fractional time must be divided into months. Finally we have the odd days left over, and doubt exists as to how they should be treated.

Before 1892 there was no doubt. The statute distinctly stated that a number of days less than a month should be estimated for interest as 30ths of a month, or, consequently, 360ths of a year. This was a most excellent provision and merely enacted what had been the custom long before. The so-called "360 day" interest tables are based upon this rule. But the revisers of the statutes of the State, in 1892, dropped this sensible provision and left the question open. No judicial decision has since been rendered on the subject, but many good lawyers think that the odd days must be computed as 365ths of a year. In business nearly every one calls the odd days 360ths, and it is only in legal accountings that there can be any question. It would be well if the old provision could be re-enacted or re-established by the courts. If it is necessary to correct the interest on the odd days from 360ths to 365ths, it may readily be done by subtracting from such interest $\frac{1}{73}$ of itself.

14.—Interest is assumed to be paid when due. If it is not so paid, it ought to be added to the principal and interest be computed on the increased principal. But as the law does not directly sanction this, *simple interest* is spoken of as if it were a distinct species, where the original principal remains unchanged, even though interest is in default. There really is no such thing, for the interest money which is wrongfully withheld by the borrower may be by him employed, and thus compound interest is earned ; only the wrong man gets it. All the calculations of finance depend upon *compound interest*, which is the only rational and consistent method. When I have occasion to speak of the interest for one period I shall call it "single interest."

15.—If we add to 1 the decimal denoting the rate, we have the ratio of increase. Thus, if the rate is .03 per period, 1.03 is the ratio of increase, or simply the ratio, or the multiplier.

16.—The Amount is the principal and interest taken together. At the end of the first period the amount of $1.00 at 3% interest is $1.03. Instead of considering the $1.00 and the 3 cents as two separate sums to be added together, it is best to consider the operation as the single one of multiplying $1.00 by the ratio 1.03.

17.—The principal which is employed during the second period is $1.03. It is evident that this, like the original $1.00, should be multiplied by the ratio 1.03. The new amount will be the square of 1.03, which we may write 1.03×1.03

or, $(1.03)^2$

or, 1.0609

This is the new amount on interest during the third period. At the end of the third period the amount will be

$1.03 \times 1.03 \times 1.03$

or, 1.03^3

1.092727

At the end of the fourth period we have reached the amount,

1.03^4

or, 1.12550881

We here find that the number of decimals is becoming unwieldy, and conclude to cut it down. If we desire to limit it to seven figures we reject the 1, rounding the result *off* to 1.1255088; if we prefer to use only six figures, we round it *up* to 1.125509, which is nearer than 1.125508.

18.—Thus the amount of $1.00 at the end of any number of periods is obtained by taking such a *power* of the ratio of increase as is indicated by the number of periods ; or by multiplying $1.00 by the ratio as many times as the number of periods. The remainder, after subtracting the original principal, is the compound interest. Thus the compound interest for four periods is .125509. The single interest is .03.

19.—The **present worth** of a future sum is a smaller sum, which, put at interest, will amount to the future sum. The present worth of $1.00 is such a sum that $1.00 will be its amount. Using the same suppositions as before we desire to find such a number as, when multiplied by 1.03, will amount to $1.00 in four periods. $1.00 must, therefore, be divided by 1.03 for the first period.

```
1.03 ) 1.00000000 ( .970873
       927
       ———
       730
       721
       ———
        900
        824
        ———
        760
        721
        ———
         390
         309
         ———
          81
```

The result, rounded up at the 6th place, is .970874, the present worth of $1 at 3% for one period, or $\frac{1}{1.03}$, or $1 \div 1.03$. The present worth for two periods may be obtained either by again dividing .970874 by 1.03, or by multiplying .970874 by itself, or by dividing 1 by 1.0609, each of which operations gives the same result, $.942596 = \frac{1}{1.03}$. The third term is $\frac{1}{1.03} = .915142$, and the fourth is $\frac{1}{1.03} = .888487$.

20.—If we arrange these four results in reverse order followed by $1 and by the amounts computed in article 17, we have a continuous series :

```
            .888487
            .915142
            .942596
            .970874
           1.00
           1.03
           1.0609
           1.092727
           1.125509
```

21.—It may be observed that each of these numbers is an *amount* of every preceding number and a *present worth* of every succeeding number, and that when one number is the amount of another, the latter is the present worth of the former ; in other words, that amount and present worth are reciprocals.

22.—Each one of these numbers may be obtained from the preceding one by multiplying by 1.03. Hence, as multiplication is easier than division, if we can obtain .88487 directly, we may supply the intermediate values more readily. This brief process for finding .88487 will be explained in the next chapter.

23.—In the present worth, .97087 of a single period, it is evident that the original \$1.00 has been diminished by .02913, which is a little less than .03 ; in fact it is .03 ÷ 1.03. This difference .02913 is called the **discount**. In the present worth for two periods the discount is 1 — .942596, or .057404. This and succeeding discounts for greater numbers of periods are **compound discounts**.

24.—Compound discount does not bear any such direct relation to compound interest as single discount does to single interest. It can only be found by first ascertaining the present worth and then subtracting that from 1.

25.—We can reduce the rules to more compact form by the use of symbols. Let s represent the amount of 1 ; p the present worth ; i the rate of interest per period ; n the number of periods, and d the rate of discount. Let the compound interest be represented by I, and the compound discount by D.

26.—Then, by article 15, the ratio of increase is $(1 + i.)$ By article 18, $s = (1 + i)^n$; and $I = s - 1$. By article 19, $p = 1 ÷ (1 + i)^n$; and $D = 1 - p$.

27.—The method of ascertaining the values of s and p through successive multiplications and divisions is, for a large number of periods, intolerably slow. A much briefer way, by the use of certain auxiliary numbers, called logarithms, will be explained in the next chapter.

CHAPTER III.

THE USE OF LOGARITHMS.

28.—For multiplying or dividing a great many times by the same number, there is no device hitherto invented which is superior to a table of **logarithms.**

29.—The use of logarithms does not require a knowledge of the higher mathematics. It is purely an arithmetical help. The popular prejudice to the effect that there is something mysterious or occult about logarithms has no foundation.

30.—The ordinary books of logarithms are calculated to 7 places of decimals, sometimes extended for certain numbers to 8. If you wished to multiply by 1.03 fifty times, the logarithm would give you the first seven figures only of the answer, but as the remaining figures are so very insignificant, the result will for most questions be near enough even if rounded off at the 6th place.

31.—All the books of logarithmic tables contain, in an introduction, rules for using the tables, and these should be studied, and the examples worked out. These books have the ordinary numbers on the left in a regular series, in four figures only ; the fifth figure is at the head of one of the ten columns to the right. The sixth and seventh figures are obtained by a little side-table.

32.—Briefly, the rules of logarithms are as follows :

By **adding** logarithms you **multiply** numbers.
By **subtracting** logarithms you **divide** numbers.
By **multiplying** logarithms you raise numbers to **powers.**
By **dividing** logarithms you extract **roots** of numbers.

33.—The last two of these rules are the only ones *necessary* to be employed in the calculations of compound interest.

34.—In the common system of logarithms 10 is the **base** ; that is, the logarithm of 10 is 1. The logarithm of 100 (being *two tens* multiplied together) is 2. The logarithm of 1,000 (in which 10 is *three* times a factor) is 3. We may thus go on in- definitely, saying in abbreviated language, log. 10,000 = 4 ; log. 1,000,000 = 6. In all these cases, the logarithm is the *number of zeroes* used to express the number. What is the meaning of these zeroes? Each of them means that ten, the base of numeration, enters once as a factor.

1,000,000 : 1 followed by 6 zeroes means
that 1 is multiplied 6 times by 10 ;
or it may be written 1 × (10) ⁶. Log. 1,000,000 = 6
Similarly .... Log. 100,000 = 5
To multiply these numbers together
you really add the logarithms, and
write 1 followed by............................11
zeroes. Thus there is a kind of
logarithmic method in ordinary
arithmetic.

35. To demonstrate the use of logarithms in compound interest, let us take an example and work it out, illustrating each step. We will take the same rate as before, .03, but endeavor to find the amount for 50 periods.

36.—The ratio of increase is 1.03. We look for the log- arithm of this ratio. At the top of page 192 (Chambers' or Babbage's tables) we find this line:

No.	0	1	2	3	4	5	6	7	8	9
10300	0128	3722	4144	4566	4987	5409	5831	6252	6674	7096	7517

37.—The meaning of this is that the logarithms are as follows :

log. 1.03	.01283722
" 1.03001	.01284144
" 1.03002	.01284566
" 1.03003	.01284987
"	....
" 1.03009	.01287517

The first figures are given once only, which saves space and time in searching.

38.—Since 1.03 is to be taken as a factor 50 times, we must multiply its logarithm by 50. This gives:

$$50 \times .01283722 = .6418610.$$

This result is the logarithm of the answer, for when we have found the corresponding number we shall know the value of 1.03^{50}.

39.—We must now look in the right hand columns for the logarithm figures .6418610. We first look for the 641, which stands out by itself, overhanging a blank space. This we find on page 73, and we find that the nearest

approach is...........................   .6418606
which is the logarithm of 4.3839.
We now, from our logarithm,   .6418610
subtract the above approximation   .6418606
and have a remainder............   04

In the margin is a little difference-table, reading thus :

	99
1	10
2	20
3	30
4	40
5	50
6	59
7	69
8	79
9	89

The left hand column represents the 6th figure of the answer. If the remainder were 10, instead of 4, the next figure would be 1 ; if it were 69, the next figure would be 7. But is less than 10, therefore the 6th figure is 0. The 7th figure is 4, because 40 would give 4 for the 6th figure.

40.—Thus we have obtained our result. $4.383904 is the amount of $1.00 compounded for 50 periods at 3%. This result is slightly inaccurate in the last figure, for the reason that two places were *lost* by multiplying. Had we taken the 10 figure logarithm on page XVIII of Chambers', .0128372247 this multiplied by 50 would give................ .641861235 or rounded off at the 7th place................... .6418612 From this subtract...................... ....6418606 and we have the remainder..................... 06 which gives the more accurate result.... ....4.383906

41.—As it is necessary, for problems involving many periods, to use a very extended logarithm, I give in Appendix 1 a table of twelve-place logarithms for a number of different ratios of increase $(1 + i)$. These are at much closer intervals than any table previously published, and, with a 10 figure book of logarithms, will give exact results to the nearest cent on $1,000,000.

42.—We will further exemplify the advantage of the logarithmic method by solving a present-worth problem. Taking 50 periods at 3% for $1.00, we discount it as follows: Multiply the logarithm of 1.03 by 50, just as in Article 40, giving .641861235. But it is the reciprocal of 1.03^{50}, or $1 \div 1.03^{50}$, which we wish to obtain; hence we must subtract .641861235 from the logarithm of 1, which is 0.

$$0.000000000$$
$$\overline{}\ 0.641861235$$
$$\text{Remainder} \quad \bar{1}.358138765$$

In subtracting a greater from a less logarithm, we get a negative whole number (as shown by the minus above), the decimal part being positive, and obtained by ordinary subtraction.

43.—Neglecting the $\bar{1}$, we search in the right hand column for .358138765. On page 31 we find that .3581253 is the logarithm of 2.2810.

From	3581388
Subtract	3581253
and we have a remainder........	135
From the marginal table we find that......	133
corresponds to 7, hence the 6th figure	
is 7, giving so far the result 2.28107.	
There is still a remainder of.............	2

which by the table is equivalent to 1 for the 7th figure. Hence, we have the full result .2281071, the decimal point being moved one place to the left, as directed by the $\bar{1}$.

CHAPTER IV.

AMOUNT OF AN ANNUITY.

44.—We have now investigated the two fundamental problems in compound interest : viz., to find the amount of a present worth, and to find the present worth of an amount. The next question is a more complex one: to find the amount and the present worth of a *series* of payments. If these payments are irregular as to time, amount and rate of interest, the only way is to make as many separate computations as there are sums and then add them together. But if the sums, times and rate are uniform, we can devise a method for finding the amount or present worth at one operation.

Annuity. A series of payments of like amount, made at regular periods, is called an annuity, even though the period be not a year, but a half year, a quarter or any other length of time. Thus, if an agreement is made for the following payments :

On Sept. 9 1904	$100.
On March 9 1905	100.
On Sept. 9 1905	100.
and on March 9 1906	100.

this would be an annuity of $200 per annum, payable semi-annually; in other words, an annuity of $100 per period, terminating after 4 periods. It is required to find on March 9, 1904, assuming the rate of interest as 6% per annum, payable semi-annually (3% per period) : First, what will be the total amount to which the annuity will have accumulated on March 9, 1906; second, what is now, on March 9, 1904, the present worth of this series of future sums. It is evident that the answer to the first question will be greater than $400, and that the answer to the second question will be less than $400.

45.—It is easy, in this case, to find the separate amounts of the payments, for the number of terms is very small, and we have already computed the corresponding values of $1.00.

The last $100 will have no accumulation, and will be
merely........................ .... $100.
The third $100 will have earned in one period, $3.00,
and will amount to......................... 103.
The second $100 will amount to 106.09
The first $100 (rounded off at cents) will amount to 109.27
and the total amount will be................. $418.36

46.—If, however, there were 50 terms instead of 4, the
work of computing these 50 separate amounts, even by the use
of logarithms, would be very tedious.

47.—Let us write down the successive amounts of $1.00
under one another:

a

Amounts of $1.

1.00

1.03

1.0609

1.092727

48.—Now, as we have the right to take any principal we
choose and multiply it by the number indicating the value of
$1.00, let us assume one dollar and three cents, and multiply
each of the above figures by 1.03, setting the products in a
second column :

a.	*b.*	*c.*
Amounts of $1.00	Amounts of $1.03	Amounts of $0.03
1.00	1.03	
1.03	1.0609	
1.0609	1.092727	
1.092727	1.12550881	

49.—Our object in doing this was by subtracting column
a from *b* to find the amount of an annuity of three cents. Before subtracting, we have the right to throw out any numbers
which are identical in the two columns. Expunging these
like quantities, we have left only the following :

a.	*b.*	*c.*
Annuity of $1.00	Annuity of $1.03	Annuity of $0.03
1.00	....	1.12550881
....	....	less 1.00
....	....	
....	1.12550881	Amount 0.12550881

That is, an annuity of *three cents* will amount, under the
conditions assumed, to twelve cents and the decimal 550881.
Therefore, an annuity of *one cent* will amount to one-third of

.12550881 or .04183627.   An annuity of $1.00 will amount to 100 times as much, or $4.183627, which agrees exactly with the result obtained by addition, in Article 45.

50.—The number .12550881 (obtained by subtracting 1.00 from 1.12550881) is actually the *compound interest* for the given rate and time, and the number .03 is the *single interest;* the amount of the annuity of $1.00 is .12550881 ÷ .03 = 4.183627.   This suggests another way of looking at it.   The compound interest up to any time is really the *amount* of a smaller annuity, one of three cents instead of a dollar, constructed on exactly the same plan, and used as a model.

51.—**Rule.** To find the *amount* of an annuity of $1.00 for a given time and rate, divide the compound interest by a single interest, both expressed decimally.

52.—Let S and P represent the amount and the present worth, not of a single $1.00, but of an annuity of $1.00, then $S = I \div i$.

53.—To illustrate, let us take the case worked out in Article 40, where we found the amount of a single dollar at 3%, for 50 periods to be......... .... 4.383906
Subtracting one dollar......... .... 1.000000
The compound interest is......... ....   3.383906
Divide this by .03 and we have........ ....112.79687
which is the amount to which 50 payments of $1.00 each, at 3% per period, would accumulate.

CHAPTER V.

PRESENT WORTH OF AN ANNUITY.

54.—To find the present worth of an annuity, we can, of course, find the present worth of each payment and add them together; but it will evidently save a great deal of labor if we can derive the present worth immediately, as we have learned to do with the amount.

55.—The like course of reasoning will give us the result. Take the four numbers representing the present worths of $1.00 at 4, 3, 2 and 1 periods respectively, and multiply each by 1.03.

a. Present Worth of Annuity of $1.00	*b.* Present Worth of Annuity of $1.03	
.888487	.915142	
.915142	.942596	
.942596	.970874	
.970874	1.000000	

Canceling all equivalents, we have

		c. Present Worth of Annuity of .03
.888487	. . . .	
. . . .	. . . .	1.000000
. . . .	. . . .	less .888487
. . . .	1.000000	.111513

Annuity of $1.00 = .111513 ÷ .03 =   3.71710

This is the same result (rounded up) as that obtained by adding column *a*.

56.—But .111513 is the compound discount of $1.00 for four periods, and we therefore construct this rule:

57.—**Rule.** To find the present worth of an annuity of $1.00 for a given time and rate, divide the compound discount for that time and rate by a single interest. Symbolically $P = D \div i$. We might give this the form $P = D \times d$, but in practice this would not be so convenient.

58.—It may assist in acquiring a clear idea of the working of an annuity, if we analyse a series of annuity payments from the point of view of the purchaser.

59.—He who invests $3.7171 at 3%, in an annuity of 4 periods, expects to receive at each payment, besides 3% on his principal to date, a portion of that principal, and thus to have his entire principal gradually repaid.

		Principal.
60.—His original principal is........		3.7171
At the end of the first period he receives 1.00		
consisting of 3% on 3.7171	.1115	
and payment on principal....	.8885	.8885
leaving new principal..........		2.8286
(or present worth at 3 periods).		
In the next instalment.....................	1.00	
there is interest on 2.8286	.0849	
and payment on principal.....	.9151	.9151
leaving new principal................		1.9135
Third instalment.........................	1.00	
Interest.................................	.0574	
on principal.........................	.9426	.9426
		.9709
Last instalment.................	1.00	
Interest.................................	.0291	
Principal in full........................	.9709	.9709

61.—Thus the annuitant has received interest in full on the principal outstanding, and has also received the entire original principal. The correctness of the basis on which we have been working is corroborated.

62.—It is usual to form a schedule showing the components of each instalment in tabular form.

Date		Total Instalment	Interest Payments	Payments on Principal	Principal Outstanding
1904	Mar. 9				3.7171
1904	Sept. 9	1.00	.1115	.8885	2.8286
1905	Mar. 9	1.00	.0849	.9151	1.9135
1905	Sept. 9	1.00	.0574	.9426	0.9709
1906	Mar. 1	1.00	.0291	.9709	0.0000
		4.00	.2829	3.7171	

Had the purchaser re-invested each instalment at 3%, he would have, at the end, $4.1836 (Article 45), which is equivalent to his original $3.7171 compounded (3.7171 × 1.1255 = 4.1836).

63.—In Article 43, using logarithms, we found the present worth of a single $1.00 at 50 periods, at 3%, to be .2281071
Subtracting this from........................ 1.0000000
we have..................................... .7718929
which is the compound discount. Dividing this by .03 we have............................ 25.72976
which is the present worth of an annuity of $1.00 for 50 periods. Thus we see that the process of finding the present worth of an annuity, or, as it is termed, evaluation, is rendered very easy, no matter how long the time, by using logarithms.

64.—The present worth of an annuity of $1.00 is sometimes called the number of years' purchase. Thus we would say, in the example just given, that a 50 year annuity, at 3%, is worth nearly 26 years' purchase ; meaning that one should pay now nearly 26 times a year's income, whatever that may be. In Hardcastle's "Accounts of Executors," page 27 and following, will be found several examples of the evaluation of leases for years, which are a species of annuity. It will be useful to work these out by logarithms to as many places as possible.

CHAPTER VI.

RENT OF ANNUITY AND SINKING FUND.

65.—The number of dollars in each separate payment of an annuity is called the rent of the annuity.

66.—We saw that 3.7171 is the present worth of an annuity composed of payments of 1.00 each. We may reverse this and say that 1.00 is the rent of 3.7171 invested in an annuity of 4 payments at 3%. What, then, is the rent to be obtained by investing $1 in the same way? Since the present worth has been reduced in the ratio of 3.7171 to 1, evidently the rent must be reduced in the same ratio, that is $1 \div 3.7171$. By ordinary division or by logarithms, this quotient is $.26903$. Therefore $.26903$ is the rent of an annuity of 4 terms at 3%, for every $1 invested. Or $1 is the present worth at 3% of an annuity of $.26903$. This may be illustrated by making up a schedule :

	RENT.	INTEREST.	REDUCTION.	VALUE.
Beginning of first period..	......	......	......	1.00000
End of first period........	.26903	.03	.23903	.76097
End of second period.....	.26903	.02283	.24620	.51477
End of third period	.26903	.01544	.25359	.26118
End of fourth period......	.26903	.00785	.26118	0.
	1.07612	.07612	1.00000	

67.—**Rule.** To find the rent of an annuity valued at $1, divide $1 by the present worth of an annuity of $1 for the given rate and time. Rent $= 1 \div P$.

68.—This may be also called finding how much per period for n periods at the rate i can be bought for $1. A borrower may agree to pay back a loan in instalments, which comprise principal and interest. Suppose a loan of $1,000 were made under the agreement that such a uniform sum should be paid annually as would pay off (amortise) the entire debt with 3% interest in 4 years. The present worth is, of course, $1,000, and by the above process each instalment or contribution would be $269.03. In countries imposing an income-tax it is usual to incorporate in the bond a schedule with columns like those in Article 66, showing what part of the instalment is interest. as that alone is taxable.

	Annual Instalment	Interest on Balance	Payment on Principal	Principal Outstanding
Jan. 1 1904..				1,000.00
Dec. 31 1904	269.03	30.00	239.03	760.97
Dec. 31 1905	269.03	22.83	246.20	514.77
Dec. 31 1906	269.03	15.44	253.59	261.18
Dec. 31 1907	269.03	7.85	261.18	0.
	1076.12	76.12	1,000.00	

69.—It may be required, also, to find such an annuity as will, at the end of a certain number of periods, have accumulated to $1.00 or any other sum. This is called a **sinking fund**, when it is intended to provide for a liability not yet matured. In the case exhibited in the schedule, in Article 68, the debt was amortised, with the assent of the creditor, by gradual payments. Let us suppose that the creditor prefers to wait till the day of maturity, and receive his $1,000 at once. He must be paid his interest of $30 each year, but the debtor, to provide for the principal, must also transfer from his general assets to a special account (or into the hands of a trustee, if he doubts his self-control), where it will draw interest at 3%, such a sum as will accumulate to $1,000. This is the sinking fund. Since $1.00, set aside, annually amounts, after 4 years, to $4.183627, to find what sum will amount to $1,000, we must divide 1,000 by 4.183627, giving for the contribution to the sinking fund $239.03.

70.—**Rule.** To find what annuity will amount to $1.00, or what should be each sinking fund contribution to provide for $1.00: divide $1.00 by the amount of an annuity. Sinking fund contribution $= 1 \div S$.

71.—If you observe the two results obtained by the two preceding rules: .26903 and .23903 you will see that they differ by .03 , which is exactly the periodical interest on the original loan. Hence the amount paid in the second case, if interest be included, is just the same as in the former. This is as it should be, for in the latter case we are investing in some other 3% security, while in the former, we are investing in part of this very obligation. Gradual payment, or gradual accumulation for a single payment, come to the same thing. These two forms of practically the same process, amortisation and sinking fund, will be useful to guide us when we study the subject of premiums on securities.

CHAPTER VII.

NOMINAL AND EFFECTIVE RATES.

72.—We have reduced all our operations to so many periods, and such a rate per period, but it is usual to speak of such a rate *per annum*, payable so many times a year, or "convertible half yearly or quarterly." Where the interest is payable otherwise than annually, the rate per annum is only nominally correct. For example: if we take 3% per half year, this would be nominally 6% per annum, but effectively it would be 6.09% per annum, because $1.03 \times 1.03 = 1.0609$. If paid quarterly, the effective rate per annum, 6.1364% would correspond to the nominal rate 6%. Evidently, the more frequent conversion results in more rapid accumulation. If paid monthly, the effective rate would be 6.1678%, while if paid daily it would be 6.1826%. But there is a limit beyond which this acceleration will not go; 6% compounded every minute, or every second, or every millionth of a second, or constantly, could never be so great as 6.184%.

73.—The process of finding the effective rate follows naturally from the ordinary rule for compound interest. If the nominal rate is 6% per annum, and it be paid quarterly, the actual ratio is 1.015, and the fourth power of 1.015 is the amount at the end of the fourth quarter, which by multiplication or by adding logarithms is found to be 1.061364, or interest .061364. It will well exemplify the logarithmic process if we apply it, finding an effective rate for daily compounding. Let the nominal interest be 6%, then the actual rate per period of a day will be $.06 \div 365$. We will first perform this division by logarithms:

Log. .06	$\bar{2}.7781513$
— Log. 365	2.5622929
Difference	$\bar{4}.2158584$

$\bar{4}.2158584$ is, we find, the logarithm of .0001643835, hence the daily ratio of decrease is 1.0001643835; and we again find the logarithm of this number, which is .00007138; 365 times .00007138 being .02605370, which is opposite the number

1.061826. If m represent the number of payments per year, and j the effective rate, we have $j = \left(1 + \frac{i}{m}\right)^m - 1$.

74.—It may also be necessary to solve another problem, in order to produce an effective rate of 6% per annum, what nominal rate is required, conversion being half-yearly, quarterly, etc. In this case we have to find the ratio of increase for the lesser unit of time, which we do by dividing the logarithm of the effective rate by the number of conversions. Thus, if we are required to find the nominal rate, which, compounded quarterly, will be equivalent to the effective rate 6%, we divide the logarithm of 1.06...................... .02530587
by 4, giving.. .... .00632647
The number opposite this is....................1.0146738
This being the quarterly ratio, the nominal annual
rate will be 4 times this rate..................... .0586952

75.—There are some other problems in compound interest, such as finding the time or the rate, when the other elements are given. But the foregoing rules will suffice for most of the purposes of investment accounts.

CHAPTER VIII.

VALUATION OF BONDS.

76.—Investments of loan-capital are usually made by means of written instruments, known as debentures or bonds. These are promises to pay: first, a principal sum at a certain date in the future; this principal sum is the par value of the bond; secondly, to pay at the end of each period, as interest, a certain percentage of the principal. The bond also contains provisions as to the time, place and manner of these payments, and usually refers, also, to the security obligated to insure its fulfillment, and to the law (in case of a corporation, public or private) which authorizes the issue. In Prof. Frederick A. Cleveland's "Funds and their Uses" will be found further particulars as to the various descriptions of bonds and similar securities.

77.—The rate of interest named in the bond is usually an integer per cent., or midway between two integers: as 2%, 2½%, 3%, 3½%, 4%, 4½, 5%, 6%, 7%. Occasionally, such odd rates occur, as 3¼%, 3.60%, 3.65%, 3¾%, but these are unusual and inconvenient. Most bonds pay interest semi-annually, and on the first day of the month. Here again there is some deviation. A considerable number of issues pay interest quarterly, and a very few annually. A very few have the interest fall due on some other day than the first of the month. These vagaries are of no benefit, and slightly injure the value of the bond. It would in some respects be better, however, if interest were payable on the *last* day of the half year, thus bringing the entire transaction inside of a calendar period.

78.—Bonds are usually designated according to the obligor, the rate of interest, the date or year of maturity, adding, if requisite, the initials of the months when interest is payable. Thus, "Manhattan 4's of '90, J & J," indicates the bonds of the Manhattan Railway Company, bearing 4% interest per annum, payable semi-annually on the first days of January and July, and payable in 1990.

79.—Bonds very frequently are bought and sold at a different price from par. This has its effect on the income derived from the investment. The amount invested being greater, the percentage of fixed income is less; beside this, the excess or premium will not be repaid at maturity, but will be sacrificed; hence, a bond purchased above par earns less than the contractual interest. Similarly, if the purchase is below par, the percentage of fixed income is greater; besides, at maturity the owner will receive not only all that he invested, but also the discount bringing it up to par. Hence a bond purchased below par earns more than the contractual interest.

80.—There are thus two rates of interest relatively to the par and the price: a nominal rate, which is so many hundredths of par; and an effective rate, which is so many hundredths of the amount invested and remaining invested. The words, nominal and effective, are as correctly applied in this case as in relation to frequency of conversion; but for the sake of distinction we shall prefer to call them the cash rate and the income rate, and designate them, when desirable, by the symbols c and i respectively. $1 + i$ is the ratio of increase as heretofore. $1 + c$ is not required, as c is not an accumulative rate, but merely an annuity purchased with the bond. The difference of rates is $c - i$ or $i - c$.

81.—The following are some of the expressions used to denote an investment made above or below par: "6% bond to net 5%;" "6% bond on 5% basis;" "6% bond yielding 5%;" "6% bond pays 5%."

82.—In a bond purchased above or below par, we have, therefore, the following elements: the par principal payable after n periods; an annuity of c per cent. of par for n periods, and a ratio of increase, $1 + i$. Given these, there are two distinct methods for finding the value of the entire security, and these must give the same result.

83.—First Method. Separate Evaluation of Principal and Annuity. Let us suppose a 7% bond, interest semi-annually, 25 years to run (50 periods), for $1,000. The present value is composed of two parts: (1) the present worth of $1,000 in a single payment, 50 periods hence; (2) an annuity of $35 for 50 terms. We can only value these when we know what is the *income-rate* current upon securities of this grade. Let us assume 3% as the income-rate per period, or what is usually called a 6% basis. The ratio of increase is 1.03.

84.—The first part of the solution is to find the present worth of $1,000 at 3% in 50 periods. In Article 42, we have found the present worth of $1.00 on the same conditions, which is .2281071; hence, the value of the $1,000 is $228.1071. It will be noticed that this result has not the slightest reference to the 7% rate of the bond. As a matter of compound interest, the 7% does not exist.

85.—We next have to value an annuity of 50 terms at $35. In Article 63, we valued a similar annuity of $1.00 and found it to be worth $25.72976. If each term be $35, the value will be $900.5417. Adding this to the value of the $1,000, we have the value of the bond, 228.1071 + 900.5417 = $1128.6488. The ordinary tables, which give the values of a $100 bond only, read 112.86, which is the same, rounded off. The above computation gives a result which is correct to the nearest cent on $100,000, viz., $112,864.88.

86.—Second Method. Division of Income and Evaluation of Premium or Discount. Each semi-annual payment of $35 may be divided into two parts: $30 and $5. The $30 is the 3% income on the $1,000; we may disregard this and consider only the $5, which is surplus interest, and, in fact, is an annuity which must be paid for in a premium. Having devoted $30 to the payment of our expected income-rate on par, we have $5, the difference of rates per period, as a benefit to be valued.

87.—We have found the present value of an annuity of $1.00 to be 25.72976. Multiplying this by 5 to get the present worth of a $5 annuity, we have $128.6488, which is the premium, agreeing with the result of the previous method. The second method is not only quicker, but it often gives one more place of decimals.

88.—In the case of a bond sold below par, the cash-rate being less than the income-rate, the same procedure is followed for finding the present worth of $5, but the result, $128.6488,

is subtracted from the par, giving \$871.3512 as the value of a
5% bond earning 6% per annum.

89.—As this second method is superior to the first, we will
adopt it as the standard.

90.—**Rule.** The premium or discount on a bond for \$1.00
bought above or below par, is the present worth of an annuity
of the difference of rates.

91.—We have found the value of a 7% bond for \$100,
paying 6% (semi-annual), 25 years to run, to be \$1128.65 to
the nearest cent. This is the amount which must be invested
if the 6% income is to be secured. At the end of the same
half year, the holder must receive 3% interest on this \$1128.65,
which is \$33.86. But he actually collects \$35, and after using
\$33.86 as revenue, he must apply the remainder, \$1.14, to the
amortisation of the premium. This will leave the value of the
bond at the same income-rate, \$1127.51. If our operations
have been correct, the value of a 7% bond to net 6%, 24½
years or 49 periods to run, will be \$1127.51. To test this, and
to exemplify the method, we will go through the entire
operation:

92.—The logarithm of 1.03 is... . ... .01283722
This × 49 =.......................... .6290238
This subtracted from 0 =..... ....$\overline{1}$.3709762
We find that the logarithm of .23495 is.......$\overline{1}$.3709754
Remainder....   8
which gives the figures 02.

Hence, .2349502 is the total discount at 3% per period for 49
periods on \$1.00. Subtracting the .2349502 from 1, we have
.7650498, which is the present value of an annuity of .03 for
49 periods. Dividing by .03 we have the present value of an
annuity of \$1.00 per period, viz., 25.50166. But the surplus
interest (35 — 30) is \$5; hence, we must multiply 25.50166 by
5, giving \$127.508, or, rounded off, \$127.51, as the premium,
at 49 periods. Adding this to the 1,000 we have \$1127.51, the
same result as in Article 91.

93.—When bonds are purchased as investment, a **Schedule
of Amortisation** should be constructed, showing the gradual
extinction of the premium by the application of surplus interest.

The following is the form recommended, but it should be continued to the date of maturity, and at intervals corrected in the last figure by a fresh logarithmic computation.

SCHEDULE OF AMORTISATION.

7% bond of the_____, payable Jan. 1, 1954. Net 6%. J J.

Date	Total Interest 7%	Net Income 6%	Amortisation	Book Value	Par
1904 Jan. 1	Cost...................1,128.65				1,000.00
July 1	35.00	33.86	1.14	1,127.51	
1905 Jan. 1	35.00	33.83	1 17	1,126.34	
July 1	35.00	33.79	1.21	1,125.13	
		etc., etc., etc.			

" Book Value " might also be termed " Investment Value."

94.—This schedule is the source of the entry to be made each half year for "writing off" or "writing up" the premium or discount, so that at maturity the bond will stand exactly at par. We give two more examples continuing them to maturity, one being above par and the other below par. As the formation of schedules is the basis of the accountancy of amortised securities, we shall present the same materials in various forms, lettering them (A), (B), etc.

SCHEDULE OF AMORTISATION (A).

5% Bond of the_____, payable May 1, 1909. M N.

Date	Total Interest 5%	Net Income 4%	Amortisation	Book Value	Par
1904 May 1			Cost	104,491.29	100,000.00
Nov. 1	2,500	2,089.83	410.17	104,081.12	
1905 May 1	2,500	2,081.62	418.38	103,662.74	
Nov. 1	2,500	2,073.26	426.74	103,236.00	
1906 May 1	2,500	2,064.72	435.28	102,800.72	
Nov. 1	2,500	2,056.01	443.99	102,356.73	
1907 May 1	2,500	2,047.13	452.87	101,903.86	
Nov. 1	2,500	2,038.08	461.92	101,441.94	
1908 May 1	2,500	2,028.84	471.16	100,970.78	
Nov. 1	2,500	2,019.42	480.58	100,490.20	
1909 May 1	2,500	2,009.80	490.20	100,000.00	
	25,000	20,508.71	4,49129		

SCHEDULE OF ACCUMULATION (B).

3% Bond of the_____, payable May 1, 1909.   M N.

Date	Total Interest 3%	Net Income 4%	Accumulation	Book Value	Par
1904 May 1			Cost	95,508.71	100,000.00
Nov. 1	1,500	1,910.17	410.17	95,918.88	
1905 May 1	1,500	1,918.38	418.38	96,337.26	
Nov. 1	1,500	1,926.74	426.74	96,764.00	
1906 May 1	1,500	1,935.28	435.28	97,199.28	
Nov. 1	1,500	1,943.99	443.99	97,643.27	
1907 May 1	1,500	1,952.87	452.87	98,096.14	
Nov. 1	1,500	1,961.92	461.92	98,558.06	
1908 May 1	1,500	1,971.16	471.16	99,029.22	
Nov. 1	1,500	1,980.58	480.58	99,509.80	
1909 May 1	1,500	1,990.20	490.20	100,000.00	
	15,000	19,491.29	4,491.29		

94.—It will be observed in these two schedules that the one is exactly as much above par as the other is below it, and that the "accumulation" and "amortisation" are exactly the same in both, being added in one case and subtracted in the other. In one line the net income is apparently in error 1 cent, but this is on account of the roundings of the fractions of a cent, and would disappear if the operation were carried to one place further.

95.—The figures in the column "Book Value" might be taken from the tables of bond values, published in book form. The column of amortisation would, in this case, be derived from the Book Values, and the Net Income from the Amortisation. The schedule would then be roughly accurate, unless the table used were carried to a greater number of places than is usually done. Sprague's Bond Tables will give eight places instead of four, and from them schedules (A) and (B) can be obtained to the nearest cent.

(C)

Date		Total Interest 5%	Net Income 4%	Amortisation	Book Value Approximate
1904 May	1				104,490
Nov.	1	2,500	2,090	410	104,080
1905 May	1	2,500	2,080	420	103,660
Nov.	1	2,500	2,080	420	103,240
1906 May	1	2,500	2,060	440	102,800
Nov.	1	2,500	2,060	440	102,360
1907 May	1	2,500	2,040	460	101,900
Nov.	1	2,500	2,040	460	101,440
1908 May	1	2,500	2,030	470	100,970
Nov.	1	2,500	2,020	480	100,490
1909 May	1	2,500	2,010	490	100,000

96.—It will be observed that in schedules (A) and (B) the entire interest is accounted for, both the interest on the par and that on the premium. We may easily construct the schedule so as to eliminate the par and its interest at the rate i, and deal only with the surplus interest or the deficient interest, according to the theory in Article 86. As this may be preferable for some forms of accounts, we again work out the schedule for "5% bond net 4%, 5 years, semi-annual":

(D)

Date		Surplus Interest 1%	Interest on Premium 4%	Amortisation	Premium
1904 May	1				4,491.29
Nov.	1	500	89.83	410.17	4,081.12
1905 May	1	500	81.62	418.38	3,662.74
Nov.	1	500	73.26	426.74	3,236.00
1906 May	1	500	64.72	435.28	2,800.72
Nov.	1	500	56.01	443.99	2,356.73
1907 May	1	500	47.13	452.87	1,903.86
Nov.	1	500	38.08	461.92	1,441.94
1908 May	1	500	28.84	471.16	970.78
Nov.	1	500	19.42	480.58	490.20
1909 May	1	500	9.80	490.20	0
		5,000	508.71	4,491.29	

97.—We have hitherto assumed that the purchase of the bond took place exactly upon an interest date. We must now consider the case when the initial date differs from the interest date. Let us suppose the purchase to take place on July 1, when one-third of the period has elapsed. The business custom is to adjust the matter as follows: The buyer pays to the seller the (simple) interest accrued for the two months, acquiring thereby the full interest rights, which will fall due on November 1, and the premium is also considered as vanishing by an equal portion each day, so that one-third of the half-yearly amortisation takes place by July 1. The amortisation from May 1 to November 1 being \$410.17, that from May 1 to July 1 must be \$136.72, and the book value on July 1 is \$104,354.57, with accrued interest, \$833.33—in all \$105,187.90. This last number is the flat price, that is to say, it is inclusive of interest. It might have been obtained in the following manner:

To the value on May 1........................\$104,491.29
add simple interest thereon, at 4%, for 2 months..   696.61
giving the flat price..................... .....\$105,187.90

In buying bonds, there is usually a stipulation that the price should be so many per cent. "and interest," otherwise the price named is understood to be "flat."

98.—This practice of adjusting the price at intermediate dates by simple interest is conventionally correct, but is scientifically inaccurate, and always works a slight injustice to the buyer. The seller is having his interest compounded at the end of two months instead of six months, and receives a benefit therefrom, at the expense of the buyer. It will readily be seen that the buyer does not net the effective rate of 4% semi-annually on his investment of \$105,187.90. The true price would be \$105,183.31, giving both buyer and seller, not 4% nominal, but the equivalent effective with bi-monthly and four-monthly conversion. In practice, however, for any time above six months, simple interest is generally used, to the slight disadvantage of the buyer, who may claim, and probably legally, that the November value + interest due should have been discounted at 4%; $106,581.12 \div 1.01\frac{1}{3} = 105,178.74$; which is almost exactly as much too low as the \$105,187.90 is too high.

99.—The schedule would, therefore, in practice, read as follows :

(E)

Date	Total Interest 5%	Net Income 4%	Amortisation	Book Value	Par
1904 July 1			Cost	104,354.57	100,000.00
Nov. 1	1,666.67	1.393.22	273.45	104,081.12	
1905 May 1	2,500.00	2,081.62	418.38	103,662.74	
Nov. 1	2,500.00	2,073.26	426.74	103,236.00	
1906 May 1	2.500.00	2,064.72	435.28	102,800.72	
Nov. 1	2,500.00	2,056.01	443.99	102,356.73	
1907 May 1	2,500.00	2,047.13	452.87	101,903.86	
Nov. 1	2,500.00	2,038.08	461.92	101,441.94	
1908 May 1	2,500.00	2,028.84	471.16	100,970.78	
Nov. 1	2,500.00	2,019.42	480.58	100,490.20	
1909 May 1	2,500.00	2,009.80	490.20	100,000.00	
	24,166.67	19,812.10	4,354.57		

100.—The interest dates may not always be the most convenient epochs for periodical valuation. There may be many kinds of bonds, the interest on some falling due in every month in the year, and yet on a certain annual or semi-annual date the entire holdings must be simultaneously valued. It will then be convenient if we can arrange our schedules so that without recalculation every book value will be ready to place in the balance sheet. Fortunately, this is easier than would be supposed.

101.—We again take a 5% bond, payable on Nov. 1, 1904, on a 4% basis, but we assume that the investor closes his books on the last days of June and December. We will suppose that the purchase is made on August 1. As this is between the May and the November periods, we must adjust the price as in Article 96, so that the August price is midway between 104,491.29 and 104,081.12, namely: $104,286.20 and interest, being the customary, not the theoretical, method. The November value need not enter into the schedule, but we must locate the December 31 value, just as we found the July 1 value in Article 96. One-third the difference between $104,081.12 and $103,662.74, or $418.38, is $139.46; 104,081.12 − 139.46 = 103,941.66. Our schedule so far reads:

Aug. 1			Cost	104,286.20
Dec. 31	2,083.33	1,738.79	344.54	103,941.66

Proceeding in the same way to find the value on June 30, 1905, from those of May 1 and November 1, we get $103,520.49.

102.—But 6 months interest at 4% on $103,941.66 is $2,078.83, which, subtracted from $2,500, gives the amortisation $421.17, and this, written off from $103,941.66, gives $103,520.49, precisely the same as obtained by interpolation between May and November. Hence we have two ways of continuing the schedule : interpolation and multiplication. In this respect the commercial practice is much more convenient than the theoretical one. Having once adjusted the value at one of the balancing periods, we can derive all the remaining by subtracting the net income from the cash interest and reducing the premium by the difference, completely ignoring the values on interest days (M & N).

103.—No difficulty arises until we reach the broken period, July 1 — May 1, 1909. Here the computation of the second column, Net Income, is peculiar. The par and the premium must be treated separately. The net income on $100,000 is taken at ⅔ of 2% for the ⅔ time, giving $1,333.33. The premium, $326.80, however, must always be multiplied by the full 2%, giving $6.54. Adding $1,333.33 and $6.54, we have $1,339.87, which, used as heretofore, reduces the principal to par. The reason for this peculiarity is that $490.20, not $326.80, is the conventional premium, on which 4% is to be computed; hence, instead of taking $3/_2$ of $326.80 for ⅔ of a period, we take $326.80 itself for a whole period, two-thirds of three-halves being unity.

(F)

Date		Total Interest 5%	Net Income 4%	Amortisation	Book Value	Par
1904	Aug. 1		Cost		104,286.20	100,000.00
	Dec. 31	2,083.33	1,738.79	344.54	103,941.66	
1905	June 30	2,500.00	2,078.83	421.17	103,520.49	
	Dec. 31	2,500.00	2,070.41	429.59	103,090.90	
1906	June 30	2,500.00	2,061.82	438.18	102,652.72	
	Dec. 31	2,500.00	2,053.05	446.95	102,205.77	
1907	June 30	2,500.00	2,044.12	455.88	101,749.89	
	Dec. 31	2,500.00	2,035.00	465.00	101,284.89	
1908	June 30	2,500.00	2,025.70	474.30	100,810.59	
	Dec. 31	2,500.00	2,016.21	483.79	100,326.80	
1909	May 1	1,666.67	1,339.87	326.80	100,000.00	
		23,750.00	19,463.80	4,286.20		

104.—In all the foregoing examples it has been assumed that the bond has been bought " on a basis," which means that the buyer and seller have agreed upon the income rate which the bonds shall pay, and that from this datum the price has been adjusted.   But in probably the majority of cases the bargain is made " at a price," and then the income rate must be found.   This is a more difficult problem.

105.—The best method of ascertaining the basis, when the price is given, is by trial and approximation — in fact, all methods more or less depend upon that,   The ordinary tables will locate several figures of the rate, and one more figure can safely be added by simple proportion.   But it is an important question to what degree of fineness we should try to attain. It seems to be the consensus of opinion and practice that to carry the decimals to hundredths of one per cent. is far enough, although in some cases, by introducing eighths and sixteenths, two-hundredths and four-hundredths may be required.   Sprague's Tables give, by the use of auxiliary figures, values for each one-hundredth of one per cent.

106.—Let us suppose that the $100,000 5% bonds, 5 years to run, MN, are offered at the round price of $104\frac{1}{2}$ on May 1, 1904.   It is evident that this is nearly, but not quite, a 4% basis. Trying a 3.99% basis we find that the premium is $4,537.39, which is further from the price than is $4,491.29, the 4% basis. Hence, 4% is the nearest basis within $\frac{1}{100}$ of one per cent.   In fact, by repeated trials, we find that the rate is about .0399812 per annum.   It is manifest that such a ratio of increase as 1.0199906 would be very unwieldy and impracticable, and that such laborious exactness would be intolerable.   Yet here we have paid $104,500, and the nearest admissible basis gives $104,491.29; what shall be done with the odd $8.71 ?   It must disappear before maturity, and on a 4% basis it will be even larger at maturity than now.   Three ways of ridding ourselves of it may be suggested.

107.—First Method of Eliminating Residues.   Add the residue $8.71 to the first amortisation, thereby reducing the value to an exact 4% basis at once.   In our example (A), instead of $410.17, the first amortisation would be $418.88.

This is at the income rate of about 3.983% for the first half year and thereafter at 4%. For short bonds the result is fairly satisfactory.

108.—**Second Method.** Divide $8.71 into as many parts as there are periods. This would give .87 for each period, except the first, which would be .88 on account of the odd cents. Set down the 4% amortisation in one column, the .87 in the next, and the adjusted figures in the third:

410.17	.88	411.05
418 38	.87	419.25
426.74	.87	427.61
435.28	.87	436.15
443.99	.87	444.86
452.87	.87	453.74
461.92	.87	462.79
471.16	.87	472.03
480.58	.87	481.45
490.20	.87	491.07

The following will then be the schedule:

(G)

Date	Total Interest 5%	Net Income 4% (−)	Amortisation	Book Value	Par
1904 May 1				104,500.00	100,000.00
Nov. 1	2,500.00	2,088.95	411.05	104,088.95	
1905 May 1	2,500.00	2,080.75	419.25	103,669.70	
Nov. 1	2,500.00	2,072.39	427.61	103,242.09	
1906 May 1	2,500.00	2,063.85	436.15	102,805.94	
Nov. 1	2,500.00	2,055.14	444.86	102,361.08	
1907 May 1	2,500.00	2,046 26	453.74	101,907.34	
Nov. 1	2,500.00	2,037.21	462.79	101,444.55	
1908 May 1	2,500.00	2,027.97	472.03	100,972.52	
Nov. 1	2,500.00	2,018.55	481.45	100,491.07	
1909 May 1	2,500.00	2,008.93	491.07	100,000.00	
	25,000.00	20,500.00	4,500.00		

109.—In example (G) the income rate varies from 3.99798 to 3.99828; hence the approximation is sufficiently close for any, except large holdings for long maturities.

110.—**Third Method.** For still greater accuracy, we may divide the $8.71 in parts *proportionate* to the amortisation. The amortisation on the 4% basis runs off $4,491.29, and we have an extra amount of $8.71 to exhaust. Dividing the latter by the former, we have as the quotient .00194, which is the portion to be added to each dollar of amortisation. With this we form a little table for the 9 digits:

```
1 0 0 1 9 4
2 0 0 3 8 8
3 0 0 5 8 2
4 0 0 7 7 6
5 0 0 9 7 0
6 0 1 1 6 4
7 0 1 3 5 8
8 0 1 5 5 2
9 0 1 7 4 6
```

From this table it is easy to adjust each item of amortisation, writing down, for example, to the nearest mill:

410.17	418.38	426.74	435.28
400.776	400.776	400.776	400.776
10.019	10.019	20.039	30.058
.100	8.016	6.012	5.010
.070	.301	.701	.200
410.97	.080	.040	.080
	419.19	427.57	436.12

The result, in schedule (H), varies at the most 5 cents.

(H)

Date		Total Interest 5%	Net Income 4% (—)	Amortisation	Book Value	Par
1904	May 1				104,500.00	100,000.00
	Nov. 1	2,500.00	2,089.03	410.97	104,089.03	
1905	May 1	2,500.00	2,080.81	419.19	103,669.84	
	Nov. 1	2,500.00	2,072.43	427.57	103,242.27	
1906	May 1	2,500.00	2,063.88	436.12	102,806.15	
	Nov. 1	2,500.00	2,055.15	444.85	102,361 30	
1907	May 1	2,500.00	2,046.25	453.75	101,907.55	
	Nov. 1	2,500.00	2,037.18	462.82	101,444.73	
1908	May 1	2,500.00	2,027.93	472.07	100,972.66	
	Nov. 1	2,500.00	2,018.49	481.51	100,491.15	
1909	May 1	2,500.00	2,008.85	491.15	100,000.00	
		25,000.00	20,500.00	4,500.00		

111.—Short Terminals. It sometimes happens (though infrequently) that the principal of a bond is payable, not at an interest date, but from one to five months later, making a short terminal period. The author has discovered a very simple method of obtaining the present value in this case. It will not be necessary to demonstrate it, but an example will test it.

112.—Suppose the 5% bond, M N, yielding 4%, bought May 1, 1904, were payable October 1, instead of May 1, 1909, or 10$\frac{5}{6}$ periods. The short period is $\frac{5}{6}$. The short ratio (4%) will be 1.0166$\frac{2}{3}$. The short interest (5%) will be .02083$\frac{1}{3}$.

We first ascertain the value for
the ten full periods, viz., for $1.. 1.0449129
Add to this the short interest... .0208333

1.0657462

and divide by the short ratio.... 1.0166667

To perform this division it will be easier to divide 3 times the dividend by 3 times the divisor.

```
3.05 ) 3.1972386 ( Quotient 1.0482750
       3.05
       ─────
        1472
        1220
       ─────
        2523
        2440
       ─────
         838
         610
       ─────
        2286
        2135
       ─────
         151
         152
       ─────
```

Multiplying down by the usual procedure, we have the following schedule:

(I)

SHORT TERMINAL.

Date		Total Interest 5%	Net come 4%	Amortisation	Book Value	Par
1904	May 1				104,827.50	100,000.00
	Nov. 1	2,500.00	2,096.55	403.45	104,424.05	
1905	May 1	2,500.00	2,088.48	411.52	104,012.53	
	Nov. 1	2,500.00	2,080.25	419.75	103,592.78	
1906	May 1	2,500.00	2,071.86	428.14	103,164.64	
	Nov. 1	2,500.00	2,063.29	436.71	102,727.93	
1907	May 1	2,500.00	2,054.56	445.44	102,282.49	
	Nov. 1	2,500.00	2,045.65	454.35	101,828.14	
1908	May 1	2,500.00	2,036.56	463.44	101,364.70	
	Nov. 1	2,500.00	2,027.29	472.71	100,891.99	
1909	May 1	2,500.00	2,017.84	482.16	100,409.83	
	Oct. 1	2,083.33	1,673.50	409.83	100,000.00	
		27,083.33	22,255.83	4,827.50		

113.—Rule for Short Terminals. Ascertain the value for the full periods, disregarding the terminal. To this value add the short interest and divide by the short ratio.

114.—It may be remarked that the same process applies to short initial periods, or even to bonds originally issued between interest dates, and also maturing between interest dates. In the latter case it would be applied twice.

115.—Discounting. Hitherto we have calculated the longest period, and then obtained the shorter ones by multiplication and subtraction. We can also work backwards, obtaining each value from the next later by addition and division. Thus, beginning at maturity with par............100,000.00
and adding to it the coupon then due.............. 2,500.00
                                                  ——————————
                                                  102,500.00
We discount this by dividing by 1.02, which gives 100,490.20
the value one period before maturity. To obtain
the next value add the coupon................. .... 2,500.00
                                                  ——————————
                                                  102,990.20
Divide again by 1.02, giving the next previous value 100,970.78
Thus successive terms may be obtained as far as desired.

116.—In the last half year of a bond, its value should be discounted, and not found as in Article 97. Thus, if the bond in question were sold, when only three months remained to maturity, $102,500 would be divided by 101, which would give $101,485.15 "flat," equivalent to $100,235.15 and interest; whereas, by the ordinary rule it would be $100,245.10. The theoretically exact value (recognizing *effective* rates, which is never done in business) would be $100,240.12. To "split the difference" would be an easy way of adjusting the matter and would be almost exact.

117.—Serial Bonds and Various Maturities. Bonds are often issued in series. For example: $30,000, of which $1,000 is payable after one year, another $1,000 after two years, and the last $1,000 30 years from date. Other series are more complex; as, $2,000 each year for 5 years, and $4,000 each year thereafter for 5 years. After finding the initial value for each instalment and adding these together, the aggregate may, for purposes of deriving successive values, be treated as a unit, and multiplied down in one process. The principles in Article

103 must be observed as to that part of the par value, if any, which comes due between balancing periods.

118.—Investment of Trust Funds. A bond which has been purchased by a trustee at a premium is subject to amortisation in the absence of testamentary instructions to the contrary. (Hardcastle on Accounts of Executors, p. 49.)

The trustee has no right to pay over the full cash interest, because he must keep the principal intact for the remainder man. If, for example, he were to invest \$104,491.29 in a 5% bond having five years to run, and the life tenant were to die at the end of five years, the fund would be depleted by \$4,491.29, to the injury of the remainder man. Since this is a 4% basis, he should pay over at the end of the first half year only 4% of \$104,491.29 (= \$2,089.83), not 5% of \$100,000 (= \$2,500). He then has \$410.17 cash to re-invest, and the fund, including this, is still \$104,491.29. It may be difficult to invest the \$410.17 at as favorable a rate as the bonds, very small and very large amounts being most difficult to invest. He can, at least, deposit it in a trust company and receive interest at some rate or other.

119.—At the end of the second half-year the bond interest is only \$2,081.62; but the beneficiary is entitled, also, to the interest on the \$410.17. If this has been re-invested at exactly 4%, the interest thereon is \$8.20, and the total payable to the beneficiary is \$2,081.62 + 8.20 = \$2,089.82, practically the same as before, and \$418.38 is deposited or invested as before. He now has in the fund \$103,662.74 + 410.17 + 418.38 = 104,491.29. He has paid over all the new interest earned, and he has kept the corpus or principal intact.

Suppose, however, he was not able to get 4% for the \$410.17, but only 3%, so that from this source would come only \$6.15, making the total income \$2,081.62 + 6.15 = \$2,087.77. There is a slight falling off in income, but that is to be expected when part of an investment is returned and re-invested at a lower rate. If the re-investment had been at 4½%, the income would have been \$2,090.74, slightly more than the first half year, owing to the improved demand for capital. It might be urged that the beneficiary ought to receive \$2,089.83 periodically — no more, no less — being 4% on

$104,491.29. This would leave $410.17 each half-year to be invested in a sinking fund, from which no interest should be drawn, but which should be left to accumulate to maturity, when it would exactly replace the premium, *if compounded at 4%*. But this hope might not be realized. Very likely the average rate would be less or more than 4%. If less, the original fund would be to some extent depleted, and the remainder man wronged; if more, there is too much in the fund, and the life tenant has received too little. It seems, therefore, that the sinking fund principle is not correct in a case like this, and that we should rather recognize a gradual disappearance of capital than constitute a fictitious sinking fund.

120.—Prof. Hardcastle's example (p. 50) expanded to $10,000 instead of $100 — would be scheduled thus:

Coupon.	Income.	Cash.	Bond.
			10,192.72
200.00	152.94	47.06	10,145.66
200.00	152.13	47.87	10,097.79
200.00	151.47	48.53	10,049.26
200.00	150.74	49.26	10,000.00
$800.00	607.28	192.72	

The life tenant would receive, at the end of the first half-year, $152.94; at the end of the second, $152.13 + whatever the $47.06 cash had earned; at the end of the third, $151.47 + whatever $94.93 had earned; at the close, $150.74 + whatever $152.46 had earned; and if the cash balance was constantly deposited in the trust company at 3%, the life tenant would receive a uniform income of $152.94.

121.—In a case reported in the State of New York (38 App. Div. 419), Justice Cullen very clearly lays down the law as to the duty of the trustee to reserve a part of the interest to provide for the premium, and says that "any other view would lead to the impairment of the principal of the trust, to protect the integrity of which has always been the cardinal rule of courts of equity." He says further: "If one buys a ten-year five per cent. bond at one hundred and twenty, the true income or interest the bond pays is not $4_{\frac{6}{10}}\%$ on the amount invested, nor 5% on the face of the bond, but $2_{\frac{7}{10}}\%$ on the investment, or $3_{\frac{24}{100}}\%$ on the face of the bond. The matter is simply one of arithmetical calculation, and tables are readily accessible, showing the result of the computation."

122.—The learned judge's example would work out in a schedule as follows, with a slight correction in the initial figures, and applying it to a par of $100,000:

Total Interest	Income Paid Over	Re-invested.	Present Value
			120,039.00
2,500.00	1,620.52	879.48	119,159.52
2,500.00	1,608.66	891.34	118,268.18
2,500.00	1,596.62	903.38	117,364.80
2,500.00	1,584.42	915.58	116,449.22
2,500.00	1,572.07	927.93	115,521.29
2,500.00	1,559.53	940.47	114,580.82
2,500.00	1,546.85	953.15	113,627.67
2,500.00	1,533.97	966.03	112,661.64
2,500.00	1,520.93	979.07	111,682.57
2,500.00	1,507.72	992.28	110,690.29
2,500.00	1,494.31	1,005.69	109,684.60
2,500.00	1,480.75	1,019.25	108,665.35
2,500.00	1,466.93	1,033.07	107,632.28
2,500.00	1,453.08	1,046.92	106,585.36
2,500.00	1,438.91	1,061.09	105,524.27
2,500.00	1,424.57	1,075.43	104,448.84
2,500.00	1,410.06	1,089.94	103,358.90
2,500.00	1,395.35	1,104.65	102,254.25
2,500.00	1,380.43	1,119.57	101,134.68
2,500.00	1,365.32	1,134.68	100,000.00
50,000.00	29,961.00	20,039.00	

123.—This is perfectly correct, but we can scarcely agree with the method described further on in the same opinion, as follows: "There is, however, a simpler way of preserving the principal intact — the method adopted by the learned referee. He divided the premium paid for the bonds by the number of interest payments, which would be made up to the maturity of the bonds, and held that the quotient should be deducted from each interest payment and held as principal. These deductions being principal, the life tenant would get the benefit of any interest that they might earn. We do not see why this plan does not work equal justice between the parties." The reason "why it does not work equal justice" is that the life tenant in the earlier years receives much less than his due share of the income, but from year to year he gradually receives more and more, until he receives more than his share, but not till the very last payment has he overtaken his true share. Thus, if he dies before the maturity of the bonds, it is certain that "equal justice" will not have been done, but the remainder man would have altogether the best of it.

124.—To particularize, the "referee's plan" would be scheduled as follows:

TRUST FUND.   "REFEREE'S PLAN."

Total Interest	Income Paid Over	Re-invested	Present Value
			120,039.00
2,500.00	1,498.05	1,001.95	119,037.05
2,500.00	1,498.05	1,001.95	118,035.10
2,500.00	1,498.05	1,001.95	117,033.15
2,500.00	1,498.05	1,001.95	116,031.20
2,500.00	1,498.05	1,001.95	115,029.25
2,500.00	1,498.05	1,001.95	114,027.30
2,500.00	1,498.05	1,001.95	113,025.35
2,500.00	1,498.05	1,001.95	112,023.40
2,500.00	1,498.05	1,001.95	111,021.45
2,500.00	1,498.05	1,001.95	110,019.45
&c.	&c.	&c.	&c.

It is unnecessary to continue this further, but by comparing it with our schedule (K) it will be seen that, if the remainder man received the fund after five years, it would be at such a valuation on the bonds that he could enjoy an income of over 2.80 per cent. for the other five years, and yet keep the principal intact. The method of the referee is false and arbitrary.

125.—Single Column Schedule. Instead of distributing the figures of the schedule into four columns, as in our examples, it is frequently easier to ignore the amortisation column and simply add the net income, then subtract the cash interest. Thus, Schedule A would begin as follows:

$$
\begin{array}{rr}
 & 104,491.29 \\
\text{plus} & 2,089.83 \\
\hline
 & 106,581.12 \\
\text{minus} & 2,500.00 \\
\hline
 & 104,081.12 \\
\text{plus} & 2,081.62 \\
\hline
 & 106,162.74 \\
\text{minus} & 2,500.00 \\
\hline
 & 103,662.74 \\
 & \text{etc.}
\end{array}
$$

The Book Values may then be set down at once; the amortisations will be their differences; and the Net Income will be the Cash Interest minus the Net Income. By using red ink for

the subtrahends (which we indicate by italic figures) setting
them down in advance on the proper lines, the addition and
subtraction can be performed at one operation. For example:

$$
\begin{array}{r}
104{,}491.29 \\
2{,}089.83 \\
\textit{2,500.00} \\
\hline
104{,}081.12 \\
2{,}081.62 \\
\textit{2.500 00} \\
\hline
103{,}662.74 \\
2{,}073.35 \\
\textit{2,500 00} \\
\hline
103{,}236.09 \\
\text{etc.}
\end{array}
$$

It will be noticed that the computation of the interest is done
without using any other paper. Even with a fractional rate,
like that in Judge Cullen's example, 2.7% per annum, or 1.35%
per period, the 1%, the .3% and the .05% can be successively
written down direct:

$$
\begin{array}{r}
120{,}039.00 \\
1{,}200.39 \\
360.117 \\
60.019 \\
\textit{2.500 00} \\
\hline
119{,}159.526 \\
1{,}191.595 \\
357.479 \\
59.580 \\
\textit{2,500.00} \\
\hline
118{,}268.180 \\
\text{etc.}
\end{array}
$$

126.—Irredeemable Bonds. Sometimes, as in the British
Consols, there is no right nor obligation of redemption. If
the government wishes to pay off it has to buy at the market
price. There is, then, no question of amortisation; the investment is simply a perpetual annuity. The cash interest is all
revenue, and the original cost is the constant book value. If
£100 of 4% consols be bought at 96, the income is £4 per
annum; the book value is £96. As an investment of £96
produces £4, the rate of income is 4 ÷ 96 = .04⅙.

127.—Optional Redemption. Sometimes the issuer has
the *right* to redeem at a certain date earlier than the date at

which he *must* redeem. It must always be expected that this right will be exercised if profitable to the issuer; hence, bonds bought at a premium must be considered as maturing, or reaching par, at the earlier date. Bonds bought at a discount must be considered as running to the longer date.

The option of redemption is sometimes attended by a premium. For example: the issuer of a thirty-year bond reserves the right to redeem after twenty years at 105. Unless you buy at such a basis that after ten years the book value will be 105 or more, this redemption right is a detriment. You must, in that case, consider that you are buying a twenty-year bond, and that the par is 1.05 times the nominal par.

There is also a form of bond-issue, not uncommon in Europe, where a certain or indefinite number of bonds is drawn by lot each year to be paid off. As they are usually issued at a discount, the earlier drawn bonds are the more profitable. The investor, in estimating his income, must assume that his bonds will be the last ones drawn. If drawn earlier, there is a profit exactly the same as that arising from a sale above book value.

NOTE.—When quarterly bonds are offered in competition with those on which interest is paid half-yearly, it is desirable to know how much is added to the value by the fact of quarterly conversion. For this purpose Appendix 2 gives a series of multipliers — decimal fractions by which the *premium* or *discount* is multiplied to give the increment thus added to the value of a semi-annual bond. At the resulting price the quarterly bond will pay an effective income equivalent to that of the semi-annual bond. Thus, a 3½% bond 35 years, yielding 2½% income, payable semi-annually, is worth 1.23234838; the premium is .23234838. In Appendix 2, on the line 2.50, in the column 3½, we find the multiplier .0109035, by which we multiply .23234838, giving .00253341 as the increment. This, added to 1.23234838, makes 1.23488179 as the value of a quarterly bond, which will be exactly as profitable as the semi-annual bond at 1.23234838. If the same bond were to yield 4½%, we have the value for semi-annual interest .82458958, or a discount of .17541042, which is multiplied by the decimal .019578, giving the increment .00343419, and the value of the quarterly bond, .82802377 (= .82458958 + .00343419).

Appendix 3 gives in condensed and progressive form the processes explained in the previous chapters.

CHAPTER IX.

FORMS OF ACCOUNT — GENERAL PRINCIPLES.

128.—In any system of accountancy on an extensive scale, in order to fulfill the opposite requirements of minuteness and comprehensiveness, it is necessary to keep, in some form, a **General Ledger** and various **Subordinate Ledgers.** Each account in the General Ledger, as a rule, comprises or summarizes the entire contents of one Subordinate Ledger. The General Ledger accounts deal with whole classes of like nature; the Subordinate Ledger with each individual asset or liability, or with groups which may be treated as individuals. It is the province of the General Ledger to give information in grand totals as an indicator of tendencies; it is the function of the Subordinate Ledger to give every desired information as to details even beyond the figures required for balancing — facts not of numerical accountancy only, but descriptive, cautionary, auxiliary. Thus the General Ledger may contain an account, "Mortgages," which will show the increase and decrease of the amount invested on mortgage, and the resultant or present amount; the Mortgage Ledger will contain an account for each separate mortgage, with additional information as to interest, taxes, insurance, title, ownership, security, valuation, and any thing useful or necessary to be known.

129.—We shall assume that a General Ledger exists with Subordinate or Class Ledgers. We shall also assume that the accounts are to be so arranged as to give currently the amount of interest earned and accruing, the amount which has accrued up to any time, and the amount outstanding and overdue at any time. It hardly seems necessary to argue this point, were it not that many important investors pay no attention to interest until it matures, and some do not carry it into account until it is paid. They are compelled to make an adjustment on their periodical balancing dates "in the air," compiling it from various sources without check, which seems as crude as it would be to take no account of cash, except by counting it occasionally.

The Profit and Loss account depends for its accuracy upon the interest earned, not upon the interest falling due, nor upon the interest collected, and the accruing of interest is a fact which should be recognized and recorded.

130.—In considering the forms of account for investments, we will first take up, as being simpler, those in which there is never any value to be considered other than par, such as direct mortgages and loans upon collateral security. Both of these classes of investment are for comparatively short terms, and are usually the result of direct negotiation between borrower and lender, not the subject of purchase and sale; hence, changes in rate of interest are readily effected by agreement, and do not result in a premium or discount.

CHAPTER X.

REAL ESTATE MORTGAGES.

131.—The instruments which we have spoken of as "bonds" are very often secured by a mortgage of property. But one mortgage will secure a great number of bonds, the mortgagee being a trustee for all the bondholders. The instruments of which we now speak are the ordinary "**bond and mortgage,**" by which the investor receives from the borrower two instruments: the one an agreement to pay, and the other conferring the right, in case default is made, to have certain real estate sold, and the proceeds used to pay the debt. As only a portion of the value of the real estate is loaned, the reliance is primarily on the mortgage rather than on the bond. Therefore, the mortgagee must be vigilant in seeing that his margin is not reduced to a hazardous point. This may happen by the depreciation of the land for various economic reasons; by the deterioration of the structures thereon, through time or neglect; by destruction through fire or by the non-payment of taxes, which are a lien superior to all mortgages. By reason of these risks a mortgage loan is seldom made for more than a few years; but after the date of maturity, extensions are made from time to time; or, even more frequently, without formal extension, it is allowed to remain "on demand," either party having the right to terminate the relation at will. A large proportion of outstanding mortgages are thus "on sufferance," or payable on demand. The market rate of interest seldom causes the obligation to change hands at either a premium or a discount, hence we may ignore that feature, referring the exceptional cases, where it occurs, to the analogy of bonds.

The two instruments, bond and mortgage, relate to the same transaction, are held by the same owner, and for most purposes are treated as a unit. In bookkeeping, the investment must likewise be treated as a unit, both as to principal and income.

132.—It is desirable to know at any time how much is due on principal, allowing for any partial payments. It is also desirable to know what interest, if any, is due and payable, and to be able to look to its collection. An account of principal and an account of interest are, therefore, requisite. It is better, however, that these two accounts for the same mortgage be adjacent.

133.—Accrued interest need not be considered as to each mortgage. It should be treated in bulk, as the revenue of the aggregate mortgages, as will be explained hereafter. The Interest account here referred to is debited on the day when the interest becomes a matured obligation, and credited when that obligation is discharged.

134.—Those who adhere to the original form of the Italian ledger will probably be averse to combining with the ledger-account any general business information; in fact, that form is not suited for such purposes, and is not adapted to containing anything but the bare figures that will make the trial-balance prove. But the modern conception of a ledger is broader and more practical: it should be an encyclopedia of information bearing on the subject of the account; it should be specialized for every class-ledger; it should be of any form which will best serve its purposes, regardless of custom or tradition.

135.—The form of mortgage-ledger which seems to the author to be the best, contains four parts : 1. Descriptive. 2. Account of principal. 3. Account of interest. 4. Auxiliary information. These may occupy four successive pages, or two pages, if preferred. In the latter case, if kept in a bound volume, the arrangement whereby two of these parts should be on the left-hand page and two on the right, confronting each other, is a convenient one, giving all the facts at one view. For a loose-leaf ledger the order 1, 2, 3, 4 will generally be found the best.

136.—Mortgages should be numbered in chronological order, and every page or document should bear the number of the mortgage loan to which it refers.

137.—The account of principal (Part 2) may be in the ordinary ledger form; but what is known as the balance column, or three column form, will be found more convenient. It contains but one date column, so that successive transactions, whether payments on account, or additional sums loaned, appear in their proper chronological order.

138.—The mortgage usually contains clauses which permit the mortgagee, when the mortgagor fails to make any payment for the benefit of the property, like taxes and insurance premiums, to step in and advance the money, which he has the right to recover with interest. It will be useful to have columns, also, for these disbursements and their reimbursements. The complete Part 2 will then take the form shown on page 62.

139.—The Interest account (Part 3) may be very simple. It contains two columns, one for debits on the day when interest falls due, the other for crediting when it is collected. The entries in the Interest account will naturally be much more numerous than in the Principal account; hence, this pair of columns may be repeated several times. The arrangement shown on page 63 has been found advantageous.

140.—Experience shows that the safest way to ensure attention to the punctual and accurate collection of interest is to charge up, systematically, under the due date, every item, and let it stand as a debit balance until collected. Many attempt to accomplish the same purpose by merely marking "paid" on a list, but this is apt to lead to confusion, and it is difficult afterward to verify the state of the accounts on any given date.

141.—It is not proposed in this treatise to prescribe the forms of Posting Medium (Cash Book, Journal, etc.) from which the postings in the ledger are made, because these forms are, in recent times, so largely dependent upon the peculiarities of the business, and have deviated so far from the traditional Italian form, that no universal type could be presented. We shall, however, give the debit and credit formulas underlying the postings, and will suggest auxiliary books or lists for making up the entries.

142.—The formula for the "Due" column of the Interest account is:

Interest Due / Interest Accrued $.................

It is a transfer from one branch of Interest Receivable, viz., that which is a debt, but not yet enforceable, to another branch, viz., that which is a matured claim.

143.—In the General Ledger the entry will be simply as above:

Interest Due / Interest Accrued $............

and this may be a daily, a weekly, a monthly entry, or for any other space of time, according to the general practice of the business; the monthly period is most in use, and we shall take that as the standard. The credit side of the entry (/ Interest Accrued) is not regarded in the Subordinate Ledger (Article 130), but the debit entry (Interest Due /) must be somewhere analysed into its component parts; in other words, there must be somewhere a list, the total of which is the aggregate falling due on *all* mortgages, and the items of which are the interest falling due on *each* mortgage.

144.—The following headings will suggest the requirements for such a list, the form to be modified to conform to the general system.

REGISTER OF INTEREST DUE.

MORTGAGES.

Date	No.	Principal	Rate	Time	Interest	Total

145.—Part 1 of the Mortgage account is descriptive. Its elements may be placed in various orders of arrangement. It is believed that the form on page 61 combines all the particulars ordinarily required in the State of New York.

146.—Part 4 is not an essential feature, and may be replaced by card-lists, if preferred. Yet, if there be space, there are advantages in having all the information about a certain mortgage accessible at one time, and concentrated in one place. The changing names and addresses of the mortgagors and owners, and the successive policies of insurance require for their record considerable space, which may be arranged under the headings on page 64.

147.—The card-form of Mortgage Ledger is also very convenient in many respects, and the forms here given may be rearranged so as to suit different sizes of cards. Both in cards

No.

MORTGAGE ON PROPERTY SITUATED

	VALUATIONS		
Date	Land	Improvements	Total

Section No..........
Ward No..........
Block No..........
Lot No..........
Map No..........
Recorded..........19..
Liber No..........
Page No..........

Attorney's No.......... Discharged..$..........19.. by..........

Improvements

Bond of .... Executed 19
Mortgage also signed by .... Due 19
Assignments, (a)

Title Policy No. .... Additional Papers

Application accepted .... 19 , Minute Book No. .... , page .... Rate of Interest,

REMARKS OR MEMORANDA

TAXES PAID

1901	1906	1911	1916
1902	1907	1912	1917
1903	1908	1913	1918
1904	1909	1914	1919
1905	1910	1915	1920

No.

LOAN TO

DATE	PRINCIPAL			INSURANCE PREMIUMS TAXES AND OTHER DISBURSEMENTS	
	LOANED	PAID IN	BALANCE	ADVANCED	REFUNDED

INTEREST ACCOUNT MORTGAGE No.

RATE

DATE	DUE	PAID	DATE	DUE	PAID	DATE	DUE	PAID

LOAN TO

No.

	ADDRESSES FOR SENDING INTEREST NOTICES.			INSURANCE				
	DATE	OWNER OR AGENT	ADDRESS	COMPANY	POLICY No.	AMOUNT	EXPIRATION	RENEWED TO

and loose leaves it will be helpful to use different colors for pages of different contents. Where interest on different mortgages falls due in different months, tags marked "J J," "F A," "M S," "A O," "M N," "J D," may project from the interest-sheet like an index, the tags of each month at the same distance from the top. This will greatly facilitate the compiling of the Register of Interest Due.

148.—The Interest Register should always be made up and proved (subject to modifications) in advance. In doing this, instead of making the computations in the register and posting thence to the ledger, a surer way is by "reverse posting"; that is, making the computation from the data in the ledger and entering it there at once, in pencil if preferred; then copying the items into the register, where the total can be proved. When this has been done, we can be sure without further check that the ledger is correct.

149.—It is desirable, also, to have receipts prepared in advance ready for signature. The correctness of these receipts may be assured by introducing them into the "reverse posting" process, as follows : Having made the computation on the ledger, prepare the receipts *from* the ledger, copying down the figures just as they appear; from the receipts make up the register, which prove as before. This method may be extended to the notices, if any are sent to the mortgagors, the notice being derived from Ledger account, the receipt from the notice, and the register from the receipt; if the register proves correct, the correctness of its antecedents is established. These interest notices may be made of assistance in the book-keeping, if their return is insisted upon and made convenient. Below the formal notification of the sum falling due on such a date, with all particulars, is a blank form something as follows :

"In payment of the above interest I inclose check on the

....*for $*................................*and*

request you to acknowledge receipt as below.

(Signature)..

Address .... *"*

The notice upon its being received, together with the check, becomes a "voucher-with-cash," and the credits on the cash book, and the interest page of the Mortgage Ledger are made directly from the documents. Book-to-book posting, which formerly was the only method of re-arranging items, is becoming obsolete, being superseded in many businesses by voucher or document posting. By the carbon process the notice and the receipt may be filled in simultaneously in fac-simile.

150.—General Ledger, Mortgages Account. The Class account "Mortgages" in the General Ledger is simply kept to show aggregates. Its entries are, as far as possible, monthly, the posting-mediums being so arranged as to give a monthly total of the same items which have already been posted in detail to the Mortgage Ledger. The standard form of Ledger account may be used, or the three column. In the former, the debits and credits of the same month should be kept in line, even though one line of paper be wasted.

[FORM 1.]

Dr.　　　　　　　　MORTGAGES.　　　　　　　　*Cr.*

1904									
Jan.	0	Balance	169,000	00	Jan.	1-31	Total paid in	7,000	00
"	1-31	Total loaned	12,000	00					
Feb.	1-29	" "	10,000	00					
March	1-31	" "	50,000	00	March	1-31	" " "	32,000	00
April	1-30	" "	20,000	00	April	1-30	" " "	40,000	00
May	1-31	" "	5,000	00	May	1-31	" " "	12 0 0	00
June	1-30	" "	10,000	00	June	1-30	" " "	3 000	00
					"	30	Balance	182,000	00
			276,000	00				276,000	00
July	0	Balance	182,000	00					

[FORM 2.]

MORTGAGES.

1904			DR.		CR.		BALANCE	
Jan.	0						169,000	00
"	— —	Transactions for month	12,000	00	7,000	00	174,000	00
Feb.	— —	" " "	10,000	00			184,000	00
March	— —	" " "	50 000	00	32 000	00	202,000	00
April	— —	" " "	20,000	00	40,000	00	182,000	00
May	— —	" " "	5,000	00	12,000	00	175,000	00
June	— —	" " "	10,000	00	3,000	00	182,000	00
		Transactions for half year	107,000	00	94,000	00	+ 13,000	00
July	0						182 000	00

151.—In order to keep the fullest control of the interest accruing and falling due periodically, it is useful to keep tabular registers, classifying the mortgages, *first*, by rates of interest; and *second*, by the months in which the interest comes due. Those investors who require all interest to be paid at the same date can dispense with the latter. The two presentations or *developments* may be on opposite pages, both proved by the same totals.

MORTGAGES CLASSIFIED BY RATES OF INTEREST.

Date	Total	Changes	3½%	4%	4½%	5%	6%
1904 Jan.	169,000		11,000	43,000	50,000	60,000	5,000
	7,000	262 —		7,000			
	162,000						
	12,000	984 +			12,000		
Feb.	174,000		11,000	36,000	38,000	60,000	5,000

MORTGAGES CLASSIFIED BY DATES.

Date	Total	Changes	J J	F A	M S	A O	M N	J D
1904 Jan.	169,000		23,000	30,000	4,000	8,000	90,000	14,000
	7,000	262 —						7,000
	162,000							
	12,000	984 +		12,000				
Feb.	174,000		23,000	42,000	4,000	8,000	90,000	7,000

The numbers in the column headed "Changes" are the serial numbers of the respective Mortgages.

CHAPTER XI.

LOANS ON COLLATERAL.

152.—Short-time investments are often made upon the security or pledge of bonds, stocks, goods or other personal property valued at more than the amount of the loan. Frequently these are payable on demand, and are known as "call-loans." It is evident that the rate of interest may be readjusted every day, or as often as either party is dissatisfied, and, if an agreement cannot be reached, the loan will be paid off. Hence, no premium nor discount will occur in this kind of investment, and, as in the case of mortgages, we need only concern ourselves with principal (at par) and interest.

153.—The accountancy of loans is even simpler than that of mortgages, and we need only give three models, for Principal account, Interest account, and Register of Collateral. The latter, at least, is often kept on cards or on envelopes, and there is great danger of the history becoming confused and unintelligible through erasures and changes in the amounts of collateral, when substitutions are made. When part of a certain security is withdrawn, the entire line should be ruled out, and the reduced quantity re-written on a new line. When a card becomes at all complicated, it is better to insert a fresh one, re-writing all collateral, but keeping the former card with it until the loan is entirely liquidated.

154.—The Interest account may be kept concurrent with the Principal account — that is, using up the same number of lines in each. In the suggested form there is a column for interest accrued as well as for interest due. The interest accrued column is merely a preparatory calculation column entered up at each change of rate or principal, so that there may be only one computation to make when the interest becomes due. With this exception the mechanism of the Loan Ledger is the same as that of the Mortgage Ledger, and the General Ledger account of loans will be similar to that of mortgages.

155.—As the principal and the interest in bond accounts are so intimately connected, it will be advisable to consider the account of interest-revenue more fully before taking up the subject of bond accounts.

LOAN TO

No.

	PRINCIPAL				INTEREST			
19	Vo'ch'r	Loaned	Paid Off	Balance	Rate	Accrued	Due	Collected

COLLATERAL SECURITY.

LOAN No.

Date Received	Par	Description	Value	Date Returned

CHAPTER XII.

INTEREST ACCOUNTS.

156.—Interest is **earned** and **accrues** every day; then, at convenient periods, it **matures** and becomes collectible; then or thereafter it is collected and takes the form of cash. These three stages may be represented by the book-keeping formulas:

1. Interest Accrued | Interest-Revenue.
2. Interest Due | Interest Accrued.
3. Cash | Interest Due.

Frequently we see the three accounts, Interest-Revenue, Interest Accrued and Interest Due, are confused under the one title "Interest," although they have three distinct functions. 1. Interest-Revenue (which alone may be termed simply "Interest") shows how much interest has been earned during the current fiscal period. 2. The balance of Interest Accrued shows how much of those earnings and of previous earnings has not yet fallen due. 3. The balance of Interest Due shows how much of that which has fallen due remains uncollected.

157.—The first of the three entries in Article 149 is the only one which imports a modification in the wealth of the proprietor; the other two are merely permutative, representing a shifting from one kind of asset to another. It is not the mere collecting of interest which increases wealth; nor is it merely the coming-due of the interest: it is the earning of it from day to day.

158.—Interest Accrued need not, and cannot conveniently, be computed on each unit of investment, as we have already stated. But it can readily be computed on all investments of the same kind and rate of interest, and the aggregate (say for a month) will be the amount of the entry "Interest Accrued / Interest-Revenue." Or a **daily rate** for the entire investments (or entire class) may be established, and this is used without change, day after day, until some change in the principal or in the rate causes a variation of the daily increment. The most complete and accurate method is to keep a double register of interest earned: *first*, by daily additions; *second*, by monthly aggregates, classified under rates and time.

159.—To exemplify this, we will take a period of ten days instead of a month, and assume that the investments are in mortgages only. On the first day of the period there are $100,000 running at 4%, $60,000 at 4½%, and $150,000 at 5%. On the second day, $10,000 at 4% is paid off, and on the fifth day $5,000 at 5%. On the seventh day a loan of $15,000 is made at 4½%, and one of $6,000 at 5%.

160.—We begin by establishing the daily rate as follows:

One day at 4% on $100,000......11.11,11
One day at 4½% on $ 60,000...... 7.50
One day at 5% on $150,000......20.83,33
Daily rate.......... .39.44,44

161.—The decimals are carried out two places beyond cents, and only rounded in the total. The Daily Register will then be conducted as follows:

DAILY REGISTER OF INTEREST ACCRUING.

Date	No.	Principal Less	Principal More	Rate		
1						39.44,44
2	647	10,000		4	39.44,44	39.44,44
"					1.11,11	
3						38.33,33
4						38.33,33
5	453	5,000		5	38.33,33	38.33,33
"					69.44	
6						37.63,88
7	981		15,000	4½	37.63,88	37.63,88
"	982		6,000	5	1.87.5	
"					.83,33	
8						40.34,72
9						40.34,72
10						40.34,72
		15,000	21,000			390.21
		Balances	at Close		Proof of Rate	
		90,000		4	One day	10.
		75,000		4½		9.37,5
		151,000		5		20.97,22
			316,000			40.34,72

162.—The Monthly Register or Summary takes up, first, the mortgages upon which payments are made, then those remaining to the end of the month, whether old or new. Its result will corroborate that of the Daily Register.

MONTHLY SUMMARY OF INTEREST ACCRUING.

Date	No.	Paid off	Remaining	Rate	Days	
2	647	10 000		4	2	2.22,22
5	453	5,000		5	5	3.47,22
7	981		15,000	4½	3	5.62,5
"	982		6,000	5	3	2.50
10			90,000	4	10	100.00
"			60 000	4½	10	75.00
"			145,000	5	10	201.38,88
			316 000			390.21

163.—The Daily and Monthly Registers of Interest Earned may be in separate books or in one book—preferably the latter in most cases. A convenient arrangement would be to use two confronting pages for a month, one and one-half for the daily, and one-half for the monthly.. If an accurate daily statement of affairs is kept, probably the Daily Interest Accrued will form part of that system. Again, the interest on Mortgages, on Bonds, on Loans, on Discounts, may be separated or be all thrown together. In all such respects the individual circumstances must govern, and no precise forms can be prescribed. Our main contention is that in some manner interest should be accounted for **When Earned** rather than **When Collected, or When due.**

164.—The General Ledger accounts of Interest, Interest Accrued and Interest Due will now be exemplified in simple form as to mortgages only. It is easier to combine the several kinds of interest, when carrying them to the Profit and Loss account, than to separate them if they are all thrown in together at first.

INTEREST REVENUE.

MORTGAGES.

1904 June	30	Carried to Profit and Loss	4270	60	1904		Total Earnings		654	58
					Jan.	1-31			654	58
					Feb.	1-28	"	"	708	25
					March	1-31	"	"	723	33
					April	1-30	"	"	756	67
					May	1-31	"	"	719	44
					June	1-30	"	"	708	33
			4270	60					4270	60

INTEREST ACCRUED.

MORTGAGES.

1904									
Jan.	0	Balance	2362	50					
	1-31	Earnings	654	58	Jan.	1-31	Due	1272	50
Feb.	1-28	"	708	25	Feb.	1-28	"	125	00
March	17	Cash for Accrued							
		on No. 987	58	33					
	1-31	Earnings	723	34	March	1-31	"	875	00
April	1-30	"	756	67	April	1-30	"	625	00
May	1-31	"	719	44	May	1-31	"	1200	00
June	1-30	"	708	33	June	1-30	"	65	00
						30	Balance	2528	94
			6691	44				6691	44
July	0	Balance	2528	94					

INTEREST DUE.

MORTGAGES.

1904									
Jan.	0	Balance	125	00					
	1-31	Due	1272	50	Jan.	1-31	Collections	1325	00
Feb.	1-28	"	125	00	Feb.	1-28	"	197	50
March	1-31	"	875	00	March	1-31	"	850	00
April	1-30	"	625	00	April	1-30	"	600	00
May	1-31	"	1200	00	May	1-31	"	1200	00
June	1-30	"	65	00	June	1-30	"	100	00
						30	Balance	15	00
			4287	50				4287	50
July	0	Balance	15						

165.—There is one entry in Interest Accrued account which does not arise from earnings : the accrued interest on Mortgage No. 987, which is paid for in cash on March 17, the mortgage not having been made direct, but purchased from a previous holder. This case occurs frequently in Bond accounts, but not so often in Mortgages.

CHAPTER XIII.

BONDS AND SIMILAR SECURITIES.

166.—The investments heretofore considered are interest bearing, but bear no premium nor discount; the variation from time to time is in the rate of interest, while the principal is invariable. When we consider investments whose price fluctuates, while the cash rate of interest is constant, the problem is more difficult, because there are several prices which it may be desired to record, viz., the original cost, the market value, the par and the book value or amortised value. The original cost and the par are the extremes: one at the beginning, and one at the end of the investment. The book values are intermediate to these, and represent the investment value, falling or rising to par by a regular law, which maintains the net income at the same rate. The market value is not an investment value, but a commercial one; it is the price at which the investor *could* withdraw his investment, but until he has done so, he has not profited by its rise, nor lost by its fall. So long as he retains his investment, the market value does not affect him nor should it enter into his accounts. It is valuable information, however, from time to time, if he has the privilege of changing investments, or the necessity of realizing.

167.—The account of principal, showing at each half year the result of amortisation, is very suitably kept in the three-column or balance-column form recommended in Article 134 for mortgages. Thus, the history of the bonds in Schedule G would be thus recorded in ledger form:

$100,000 SMITHTOWN 5's OF MAY 1, 1914.

Date		Dr.	Cr.	Balance
1904 May 1	Purchased from A. B. & Co.	104,500		
Nov. 1	Amortisation (4%)		410.97	104,089.03
1905 May 1	" "		419.19	103,669.84
Nov. 1	" "		427.57	103,242.27
1906 May 1	" "		436.12	102,806.15

168.—In case of an additional purchase the account will, of course, be debited and cash credited. It will then be necessary to reconstruct the schedule from that point on. This may be done in either of two ways: 1. Make an independent schedule of the new purchase, and then consolidate this with the old one, adding the terms. 2. Add together the values of the old and new bonds at the next balance date; find what the basis of the total is, eliminate any slight residue (Articles 106, 107, 108), and proceed with the calculation.

169.—In case of a sale, the procedure is different. Instead of crediting the Bond account by cash, it is best to transfer the amount sold to a **Bond Sales** account at its book value computed down to the day of sale; Bond Sales account will then show a debit, and the cash proceeds will be credited to the same account. The resultant will show a gain or loss on the sale, and at the balancing date the account will be closed into Profit and Loss. Thus, in the example in Article 165, we will suppose a sale on August 1, 1906, of half the $100,000 at 102.88, or $51,440. We find the book value of the $50,000 on August 1, which is $51,291.86; we transfer this to the debit of the Bond Sales account in the General Ledger, which account we credit with the $51,440 cash proceeds. Bond Sales is purely a Profit and Loss account, and at the proper time will show the actual profit realized on the sale, $51,440 — $51,291.86 = $148.14.

(BOND LEDGER.)

$100,000 SMITHTOWN 5's OF MAY 1, 1914.

Date		Dr.	Cr.	Balance
1904 May 1	Purchased of A. B. & Co.	104,500		
Nov. 1	Amortisation		410.97	104,089.03
1905 May 1	"		419.19	103.669.84
Nov. 1	"		427.57	103.242.27
1906 May 1	"		436.12	102,806.15
Aug. 1	Sale to C. D. & Co.			
	$50,000 @ 102.88		51,291.86	51,514.29
"	Amortisation on $50,000		111.21	51,403.08
Nov. 1	" on balance		222.43	51,180.65

(GENERAL LEDGER.)

BOND SALES.

1904 Aug. 1	Smithtown 5's	51,291.86	Aug. 1	Proceeds	51,440.00

To adjust the profit on the Bond account itself would be as unphilosophical as the old-fashioned Merchandise account before the Sales account was introduced, and even more awkward.

170.—Besides the book value, the par is also needed because the cash interest is reckoned upon the par. For some purposes, also, the original cost is useful to be shown. We must, therefore, provide means for exhibiting these three values: the par, the original cost and the book value. A mere memorandum of par and cost at the top would be sufficient where the group of bonds in question will all be held to the same time; but this is not always the case, and provision must be made for increase and decrease. The three-column form of ledger spoken of in Article 158, constantly exhibiting the balance, is the most suitable for this purpose also. But if we endeavor to display all of these forms side by side, we require nine columns, and this makes an unwieldy book. I have, therefore, come to the conclusion that the most practical way is to abandon the use of debit and credit columns, and proceed by addition and subtraction, or in what the Italians term the *scalar* (ladder-like) form, which gives a perfectly clear result, especially if the balances are all written in red. Headed by a description of the bonds, and embracing, also, a place for noting the market value at intervals (not as matter of account, but of information) the Principal account will appear as shown on page 77.

171.—As far as the Bond Ledger is concerned, the transfer of the $50,000 sold to Sales account is final; we have, however, in the example indicated a way of incorporating a statement of the profit or loss in the margin for historical purposes. The amortisation of Nov. 1 is composed of two parts: 3 months on $50,000 sold, $111.21, and the regular 6 months on $50,000 retained, $222.43. In the example in Article 167 these are entered separately; either method may be pursued, but on the whole there are greater advantages in postponing all entries of amortisation till the end of the half year. The three months' amortisation of the bonds sold is in effect implied in the price $51,291.86 reduced from $51,403.07, the half of $102,806.15, but it need not be entered till Nov. 1.

172.—The Register of Interest Due on Bonds is conducted on precisely the same principles as that described for Mortgages

Obligation of
And issued by *The Village of Smithtown*

Name of Obligation *Sewer Bonds*
Where payable *at the First National Bank, New York*   Date *1st May, 1894*
When payable *1st May, 1914*
INTEREST at *5 %* per annum, payable each *1st of May and November*
How payable *by Coupon*   Net income *4 %*
Numbers *51 to 150*

Date	Voucher	PRINCIPAL	Par Value	Original Cost	Book Value	Market Value
1904 May 1 Nov. 1	2572	Bought from A. B. & Co. Amortisation	100,000.00	104,500.00	104,500.00 410.97	
1905 May 1		"			104,089.08 419.19	104,000.00
Nov. 1		"			103,669.84 427.57	103,875.00
1906 May 1		"			103,242.27 436.12	103,000.00
Aug. 1	J 697	Sale to C. D. & Co. for Profit 51,440.00 148.25	50,000.00	52,250.00	102,806.15 51,291.86	103,000.00
Nov. 1		Amortisation	50,000.00	52,250.00	51,514.29 333.64	
1907 May 1		"			51,180.65	51,200.00

in Article 141; in fact, they are but sub-divisions of the same
Register.   Of course, the cash interest is alone considered.

173.—The Interest pages of the Bond Ledger are also
similar to those of the Mortgage Ledger (Article 136), but the
dates of interest due may be printed in advance, there being
but little chance of partial payments disturbing their orderly
arrangement.

174.—The paging of the Bond Ledger will probably be geo-
graphical, as far as possible, in respect to public issues, and
alphabetical in respect to those of private corporations.   The
loose-leaf plan permits an indefinite number of classifications
to choose from.   The date-tags suggested in Article 144 are
especially useful for pointing out dates for interest falling
due, as "J J," "F A," etc.

175.—The entries of amortisation are made directly from
the schedules of amortisation, the preparation of which has
been fully taught in Chapter VIII.   But it is necessary, also,
to make up a list of these several amortisations in order to form
the General Ledger entry:

Amortisation / Bonds,
or, Amortisation / Premiums,

according to the form of the General Ledger.   This list should
be in the same order as the Bond Ledger.   Probably the most
practical way is to combine it with the trial-balance of the Bond
Ledger, thus giving at each fiscal period a complete list of the
holdings, which may give the par, cost, book and market values,
the titles of the securities being written but once.

BOND STATEMENT FOR THE HALF YEAR ENDING......................

Name and Description	Amorti- sation	Book Value	Par Value	Original Cost	Market Value

The total of the second column will form the entry for amortisation.   The next three columns will corroborate the General
Ledger balances.

We have provided in this form for amortisation only and not for accumulation on bonds below par. Where the latter values are few in number they may be embraced in the same column, but distinguished as negatives by being written in red or encircled. If the bonds below par are numerous there should be two columns : " amortisation " and " accumulation."

176.—While the book value is the proper one to be introduced into the General Ledger, the par is very necessary, and sometimes the cost, and these requirements inevitably introduce some complexity. There are two modes of effecting the purpose :

I. By considering the par and cost as extraneous information and ruling side columns for them beside the book value.

II. By dividing the account into several accounts, by the proper combination of which the several values may be obtained.

177.—Plan I. will preserve the conformity of the Bonds account with the Bond Ledger better than the other. The Bonds account may, if necessary, be extended across both pages of the ledger, to allow for three debit and three credit columns, if all are required.

178.— Plan II. will commend itself more to those having a repugnance to introducing into the General Ledger any figures beyond those actually forming part of the trial-balance. The theory on which it is based is that the premium is not part of the bond, but is a sum paid in advance for excess-interest, while the discount is a rebate returned to make good deficient interest. This is a perfectly admissible way of looking at the matter, especially from the personalistic point of view; for the debtor does not owe us the premium and has nothing to do with it. Still the other view, which regards the investment as a whole, is also correct, and we may adopt whichever is most suitable to our purposes.

179.—If original cost is disregarded, or deemed easily obtainable when required, the accounts may be

1. Bonds at Par.
2. Premiums.
3. Discounts.

or, 1. Bonds at Par.
2. Premiums and Discounts.

If premiums and discounts are kept separate, Premiums account must always show a debit balance, being credited for amortisation ; Discounts account must show a credit balance, being debited for accumulation.   If the two are consolidated, the net amortisation only will be credited (see Art. 173); or, if the greater part of the bonds were below par, the net accumulation only would be debited.   The choice between one account and two for premiums and discounts would be largely a question of convenience.

The management of such a double or triple account is obvious, entries of transactions being divided between par and premiums, or par and discounts, but we give on pages 83 and following, an example of each.

We shall hereafter confine the discussion to premiums, leaving the cases of discount to be determined by analogy.

180.—Where it is deemed necessary to keep account of cost also, as well as of par and book value, the difficulty is somewhat greater, as we have a valueless or extinct quantity to record, namely so much of the original premium on bonds still held as has not yet been absorbed in the process of amortisation. This carrying of a dead value, which is somewhat artificial, necessitates the carrying, also, of an artificial annulling or off-setting account, the sole function of which is to express this departed value.   We may call this credit account "Amortisation Fund."   It is analogous to Depreciation and Reserve Funds. The part of the premiums which has been extinguished by the Amortisation Fund may be designated as " Premiums Amortised," or " Ineffective Premiums," while the live premiums may be styled " Effective Premiums," being what in Art. 177 we called simply " Premiums."   A double operation takes place in these accounts : *first*, the absorption of effective premiums by lapse of time ; and *second*, the rejection of ineffective premiums upon redemption or sale.

181.—There are two ways of carrying on these accounts, differing as to Premiums.   We may keep two accounts: "Effective Premiums" and "Amortised Premiums," or we may combine these in one, " Premiums at Cost."   The entire scheme will be :   a.   Bonds at Par.
                b.   Premiums at Cost.
                     e.   Amortisation Fund.

or, a.   Bonds at Par.
    c.   Effective Premiums.
    d.   Amortised Premiums.
      e.   Amortisation Fund.

"a" will in both schemes be the same; "e" will also be the same. "b" is the sum, c+d. In the former, the cost is a+b, while the book value is a+b—e. In the latter the book value is a+c, while the cost is a+c+d. The former gives the cost more readily than the latter, and the book value less readily. The former might be considered the more suitable for a trustee; the latter, for an investor.

182.—Account *a*, Bonds at Par, is debited for par value of purchases and credited for par value of sales. Its two only entries are :

Bonds at Par/Cash.
Cash/Bonds at Par.

183.—In case of purchase at a premium, the premium is charged to Premiums at Cost or to Effective Premiums, as the case may be, there being no ineffective premium at this time.

184.—When premiums are written off, on the first plan, there is but one entry : crediting the Amortisation Fund and debiting the Profit and Loss account or its sub-division.

Amortisation/Amortisation Fund.

185.—The second plan involves not only this process, but a transfer from Effective to Amortised Premiums. Thus the aggregate of premiums written off is posted four times as a consequence of the separation of premiums at cost into two accounts :

Premiums Amortised/Effective Premiums.
Amortisation/Amortisation Fund.

186.—The word " Amortisation " has been used in the specimen entries as the title of an account tributary to Profit and Loss. At the balancing period it may be disposed of in either of two ways : it may be closed into Profit and Loss direct ; or it may be closed into Interest account, the balance of which will enter into Profit and Loss at so much lessened a figure. In the former method the Profit and Loss account will show, on the credit side, the gross cash-interest, and on the debit the amount devoted to amortisation ; the second method exhibits the net income only. Whether it be preferable to show both elements, or only the net resultant, will be determined by expediency.

187.—In Articles 169 and 171 we discussed two methods of keeping account of amortisation : the first (169), where any incidental amortisation occurring in the midst of the period is at once entered; the second, exemplified in 171, where all such entries are deferred to the end of the period, and comprised in one entry in the General Ledger.

If the latter method be adopted, the Amortisation account may be dispensed with altogether, and the total amount amortised (which is credited to Bonds, or to Premiums, or to Amortisation Fund) may be debited at once to Profit and Loss or to Interest, without resting in a special account. A single item, of course, needs no machinery for grouping.

188.—**Irredeemable Bonds** (Art. 126) merely lack the element of amortisation, and require no special arrangement of accounts. The par is purely ideal, as it never can be demanded and is merely a basis for expressing the interest paid. What the investor buys is a perpetual annuity. If he buys such annuity of $6 per annum, it is unimportant whether it is called 6% on $100 principal, or 4% on $150 principal ; and this $150 may be the par value, or it may be $100 par at 50% premium, or $200 par at 25% discount. The par value is really non-existent ; and this illustrates the absurdity of reducing even redeemable securities to par, which is practised by some investors, par being, except at the moment of maturity, an unreal sum.

189.—We will now give examples of the two plans for the General Ledger outlined in Articles 176 to 187. We will suppose that on Jan. 1, 1901, the following lots of bonds are held:

JANUARY 1, 1901.

PAR		BOOK VALUE
100,000	5% Bonds, J. J., due Jan. 1, 1911, net 2.7%; value...... original cost, 124,263.25	120,039.00
100,000	3% Bonds, M. N., due May 1, 1904, net 4%; value...... original cost, 93,644.28	96,909.10
10,000	4% Bonds, A. O., due Oct. 1, 1902, net 3%; value...... original cost, 10,250.00	10,169.19
210,000	Totals	227,117.29

The premiums on the 5% and 4% bonds amount to $20,208.19. The discount on the 3%s is $3,090.90. The net premium is $17,117.29. The total original cost was $228,157.53.

PLAN I (ART. 176) FOR GENERAL LEDGER.

Dr.   BONDS ACCOUNT.   Cr.

1901	Par	Cost		1901	Par	Cost	
Jan. 0, Balances	210,000.00	228,157.53	227,117 29	June 30, Amortisation			488.76
				Dec. 31, "			492.59
				1902			
				June 30, "			496 40
				Oct. 1, Redeemed	10,000.00	10,250.00	10,000 00
				Dec. 31, Amortisation			475.21
				1903			
				June 30, "			453.63
				Dec. 31, "			456.68
				" Balances.....	200,000.00	217,907.53	214 254.02
	210,000.00	228,157.53	227,117.29		210,000.00	228,157.53	227,117.29
1904 Jan. 0, Balances	200,000.00	217,907.53	214,254.02				

PLAN II, 1 (ART. 179), FOR GENERAL LEDGER.

Dr.   BONDS AT PAR.   *Cr.*

1901	1902
Jan. 0, Balance..........210,000.00	Oct. 1, Redeemed.......10,000.00

Dr.   PREMIUMS.   *Cr.*

1901	1901
Jan. 0, Balance...........20,208.19	June 30, Amortisation 926.94
	Dec. 31, " 939.54
	1902
	June 30, " 952.28
	Dec. 31, " 940.21
	1903
	June 30, " 927.93
	Dec. 31, " 940.47

Dr.   DISCOUNTS.   *Cr.*

1901	1901
June 30, Accumulation.......438.18	Jan. 0, Balance..........3,090.90
Dec. 31, " 446.95	
1902	
June 30, " 455.88	
Dec. 31, " 465.00	
1903	
June 30, " 474.30	
Dec. 31, " 483.79	

PLAN II, 2 (ART. 179), FOR GENERAL LEDGER.

ORIGINAL COST OMITTED.

Dr.   BONDS AT PAR.   *Cr.*

1901	1902
Jan. 0, Balance..........210,000.00	Oct. 1, Redeemed.......10,000.00

Dr.   PREMIUMS AND DISCOUNTS.   *Cr.*

1901	1901	
Jan. 0, Balance...........17,117.29	June 30, Amortisation.....488.76	
	Dec. 31, " 492.59	
	1902	
	June 30, " 496.40	
	Dec. 31, " 475.21	
	1903	
	June 30, " 453.63	
	Dec. 31, " 456.68	

PLAN II, 3 (ART. 184), FOR GENERAL LEDGER.

"BONDS AT PAR" AS IN FOREGOING PLANS.

Dr.	PREMIUMS AT COST.	Cr.

1901	1902
Jan. 0, Balance...........18,157.53	Oct. 1, Canceled at Re-
	demption.......... 250.00
	1903
	Dec. 31, Balance 17,907.53
18,157.53	18,157.53
1903	
Jan. 0, Balance...........17,907.53	

Dr.	AMORTISATION FUND.	Cr.

1902	
Oct. 1, Canceled at Re-	1901 .
demption........... 250.00	Jan. 0, Balance.........1,040.24
1903	June 30, Amortisation... 488.76
Dec. 31, Balance 3,653.51	Dec. 31, " ... 492.59
	1902
	June 30, " ... 496.40
	Dec. 31, " ... 475.21
	1903
	June 30, " ... 453.63
	Dec. 31, " ... 456.68
3,903.51	3,903,51
	1904
	Jan. 0, Balance..........3,653.51

PLAN II, 4 (ART. 185), FOR GENERAL LEDGER.

BY THE BALANCE COLUMN METHOD.

BONDS AT PAR.		Dr.	Cr.	Balance Dr.
1901 Jan. 0	Balance.................	210,000.00		
1902 Oct. 1	Redemption.............		10,000.00	200,000.00

EFFECTIVE PREMIUMS.		Dr.	Cr.	Balance Dr.
1901 Jan. 0	Balance.................	17,117.29		
June 30	Amortised..............		488.76	16,628.53
Dec. 31	"		492.59	16,135.94
1902 June 30	"		496.40	15,639.54
Dec. 31	"		475.21	15,164.33
1903 June 30	"		453.63	14,710.70
Dec. 31	"		456.68	14,254.02

INEFFECTIVE OR AMORTISED PREMIUMS		Dr.	Cr.	Balance Dr.
1901 Jan. 0	Balance.................	1,040.24		
June 30	Amortised..............	488.76		1,529.00
Dec. 31	"	492.59		2,021.59
1902 June 30	"	496.40		2,517.99
Oct. 1	Canceled by Redemption.		250.00	2,267.99
Dec. 31	Amortised..............	475.21		2,743.20
1903 June 30	"	453.63		3,196.83
Dec. 31	"	456.68		3,653.51

AMORTISATION FUND.		Dr.	Cr.	Balance Cr.
1901 Jan. 0	Balance.................		1,040.24	
June 30	Amortised.....		488.76	1,529.00
Dec. 31	"		492.59	2,021.59
1902 June 30	"		496.40	2,517.99
Oct. 1	Canceled by Redemption.	250		2,267.99
Dec. 31	Amortised..............		475.21	2,743.20
1902 June 30	"		453.63	3,196.83
Dec. 31	"		456.68	3,653.51

CHAPTER XIV.

DISCOUNTED VALUES.

190.—The securities heretofore considered have all carried a stipulated rate of interest or annuity.   There is another class in which no periodical interest attaches, but the obligation is simply to pay a single definite sum on a certain date.   The present value of that sum at the current or contractual rate of income is, of course, obtained by discounting according to the principles explained in Chapter II.   If the maturity were more than one year distant at the time of discount, it would be necessary to compute the compound discount; but in practice this never occurs, such discounts being for a few months.

191.—The obligations so treated are almost invariably promissory notes.   Formerly they consisted largely of bills of exchange, hence the survival in bookkeeping of the words " Bills Receivable," " Bills Payable " and " Bills Discounted."

192.—These obligations belong rather to mercantile and banking accountancy than to that of investment.   The arrangement of accounts for recording their amounts, classification and maturity has been so fully treated in works on those branches that we only refer to them here for the purpose of illustrating another phase of the process of securing income.

193.—The difference between the rate of interest and the rate of discount has been pointed out in Chapter II.   It was there shown (Art. 23) that in a single period the rate of interest 3% corresponds to a rate of discount .02913.   Hence, if we discount a note at .02913, we acquire interest at the rate of .03 on the .97087 actually invested. The rate of interest is always greater than the rate of discount.

It is usual to name a rate of discount rather than a rate of interest in stipulating for the acquisition of notes. For example, a three months note for $1000 is taken for discount at 6% [per annum]. This means that .015 is to be retained by the payee from each dollar and the amount actually paid over is $985. The income from this is the $15, and by dividing $15 by $985 we readily ascertain that the rate of interest realized is .0609. It is sometimes believed that there is a kind of deception in this ; that the borrower agrees to pay 6% and actually has to pay 6.09%. But this is not so : the bargain is not to pay 6% interest, but to allow 6% discount, which is a different thing.

193.—Curiously, the lawfulness or unlawfulness of a transaction sometimes depends upon the mere form of words in which it is expressed. Thus, if I lend $985 to another, who promises to repay $1000 at 3 months, if his promise reads

" I promise to pay $1000,"

I am a law-abiding citizen ; but if he writes

" I promise to pay $985 and interest at 6.09% per annum,"

the statute is violated. But it is too much to expect regard for logic in a usury law.

194.—Notes discounted are usually entered among the assets at the full face and the discount credited to an opposite account, "Discounts," the latter having precisely the same effect as the Discounts account used in connection with bonds. The difference of the two is the cost.

195.—Strictly speaking, the discount is at first an offset to the note, and represents at that time nothing earned whatever ; as time goes on, the earning is effected by diminution of this offset, which is equivalent to a rise of the net value of the note, from cost to par. We may represent the process by exhibiting the state of the accounts at the initial date and at the end of each month up to maturity, for a 3 months' note for $1000 discounted at 6%.

1. WHEN DISCOUNTED.

NOTE.		DISCOUNT.
1000.00		15.00

2. AFTER ONE MONTH.

NOTE.	DISCOUNT.		INTEREST REVENUE.
1000.00	5.00	15.00	5.00

3. AFTER TWO MONTHS.

NOTE.	DISCOUNT.		INTEREST REVENUE.
1000.00	5.00	15.00	5.00
	5.00		5.00

4. AT MATURITY.

NOTE.	DISCOUNT.		INTEREST REVENUE.
1000.00	5.00	15.00	5.00
	5.00		5.00
	5.00		5.00
	15.00	15.00	

195. Notes being for short periods, this gradual crediting of earnings is usually ignored, and the Discounts account stands unaltered until the balancing period and is then closed into Profit and Loss. As most of the notes have matured during the period, the result is correct so far as concerns those notes; but as to the notes still running there is an error, for the discount has not all been earned. It is proper to make an adjustment to correct this error, which can be done as follows:

196.—Compute interest from the balancing date to the maturity of each note on the par at the rate of discount; subtract the total from the total of Discounts account; transfer only the remainder to Interest or directly to Profit and Loss. Then balance the Discounts account, and the balance brought down will be the discounts as yet unearned. The investment value of the notes on hand will be the difference between the par and the unearned discount.

APPENDIX I.

LOGARITHMS, TO 12 PLACES, OF VARIOUS RATIOS.

RATIO	LOGARITHM	RATIO	LOGARITHM
1.005	.002 166 061 757	1.022	.009 450 895 799
1.00525	.002 274 081 775	1.0225	.009 663 316 679
1.0055	.002 382 074 933	1.023	.009 875 633 712
1.00575	.002 490 041 244	1.0235	.010 087 846 999
1.006	.002 597 980 720	1.02375	.010 193 914 768
1.00625	.002 705 893 376	1.024	.010 299 956 640
1.0065	.002 813 779 225	1.0245	.010 511 962 737
1.00675	.002 921 638 280	1.025	.010 723 865 392
1.007	.003 029 470 554	1.0255	.010 935 664 704
1.00725	.003 137 276 061	1.026	.011 147 360 776
1.0075	.003 245 054 813	1.02625	.011 253 170 127
1.00775	.003 352 806 825	1.0265	.011 358 953 707
1.008	.003 460 532 110	1.027	.011 570 443 597
1.00825	.003 568 230 680	1.0275	.011 781 830 548
1.0085	.003 675 902 549	1.028	.011 993 114 659
1.00875	.003 783 547 730	1.02875	.012 309 848 220
1.009	.003 891 166 237	1.029	.012 415 374 762
1.00925	.003 998 758 083	1.0295	.012 626 350 954
1.0095	.004 106 323 280	1.03	.012 837 224 705
1.00975	.004 213 861 842	1.031	.013 258 665 284
1.01	.004 321 373 783	1.03125	.013 363 961 558
1.0105	.004 536 317 852	1.032	.013 679 697 291
1.011	.004 751 155 591	1.0325	.013 890 060 328
1.01125	.004 858 534 621	1.033	.014 100 321 520
1.0115	.004 965 887 107	1.03375	.014 415 522 561
1.012	.005 180 512 504	1.034	.014 520 538 758
1.0125	.005 395 031 887	1.035	.014 940 349 793
1.013	.005 609 445 360	1.036	.015 359 755 409
1.0135	.005 823 753 029	1.03625	.015 464 543 558
1.01375	.005 930 867 219	1.037	.015 778 756 389
1.014	.006 037 954 997	1.0375	.015 988 105 384
1.0145	.006 252 051 369	1.038	.016 197 353 512
1.015	.006 466 042 249	1.03875	.016 511 036 792
1.0155	.006 679 927 741	1.039	.016 615 547 557
1.016	.006 893 707 948	1.04	.017 033 339 299
1.01625	.007 000 558 602	1.0425	.018 076 063 646
1.017	.007 320 952 923	1.045	.019 116 290 447
1.0175	.007 534 417 897	1.0475	.020 154 031 638
1.018	.007 747 778 001	1.05	.021 189 299 070
1.0185	.007 961 033 336	1.0525	.022 222 104 508
1.01875	.008 067 621 748	1.055	.023 252 459 634
1.019	.008 174 184 006	1.0575	.024 280 376 047
1.02	.008 600 171 762	1.06	.025 305 865 265
1.0205	.008 813 009 052	1.0625	.026 328 938 722
1.021	.009 025 742 087	1.065	.027 349 607 775
1.02125	.009 132 069 540	1.0675	.028 367 883 697
1.0215	.009 238 370 968	1.07	.029 383 777 685

APPENDIX II.

Net Income	3% Bond	3½% Bond	4% Bond	4½% Bond	5% Bond	6% Bond	7% Bond
2.50	.0186918	.0109035	.0083075	.0070094	.0062306	.0053405	.0048460
2.55	.0211827	.0117062	.0087653	.0073325	.0064845	.0055259	.0049982
2.60	.0242963	.0125981	.0092557	.0076725	.0067490	.0057168	.0051538
2.65	.0282994	.0135948	.0097825	.0080309	.0070247	.0059133	.0053129
2.70	.0336369	.0147161	.0103498	.0084092	.0073124	.0061158	.0054758
2.75	.0411092	.0159869	.0109604	.0088091	.0076128	.0063245	.0056424
2.80	.0523175	.0174392	.0116261	.0092325	.0079269	.0065397	.0058131
2.85	.0709980	.0191148	.0123475	.0096815	.0082556	.0067617	.0059867
2.90	.1083586	.0210697	.0131344	.0101586	.0085999	.0069909	.0061668
2.95	.2204401	.0233800	.0139962	.0106665	.0089610	.0072275	.0063501
3.00	....	.0261523	.0149442	.0112081	.0093401	.0074721	.0065381
3.05	.2278844	.0295406	.0159919	.0117871	.0097387	.0077249	.0067308
3.10	.1158030	.0337759	.0171560	.0124075	.0101582	.0079864	.0069284
3.15	.0784424	.0392212	.0184570	.0130737	.0106003	.0082571	.0071311
3.20	.0597619	.0464815	.0199206	.0137912	.0110670	.0085374	.0073392
3.25	.0485535	.0566458	.0215794	.0145661	.0115604	.0088279	.0075528
3.30	.0410812	.0718922	.0234750	.0154055	.0120827	.0091292	.0077721
3.35	.0357438	.0973026	.0256622	.0163178	.0126367	.0094418	.0079975
3.40	.0317407	.1481232	.0282139	.0173131	.0132253	.0097664	.0082291
3.45	.0286271	.3005843	.0312196	.0184031	.0138518	.0101037	.0084672
3.50	.0261361	....	.0348482	.0196021	.0145201	.0104545	.0087121
3.55	.0240981	.3092587	.0392710	.0209273	.0152344	.0108195	.0089640
3.60	.0223997	.1567976	.0447993	.0223997	.0159998	.0111998	.0092234
3.65	.0209625	.1059770	.0519071	.0240452	.0168217	.0115963	.0094905
3.70	.0197306	.0805666	.0613841	.0258964	.0177069	.0120097	.0097656
3.75	.0186629	.0653202	.0746517	.0279944	.0186629	.0124419	.0100493
3.80	.0177287	.0551559	.0945530	.0303920	.0196985	.0128936	.0103417
3.85	.0169043	.0478956	.1277216	.0331662	.0208242	.0133662	.0106435
3.90	.0161715	.0424503	.1940585	.0363860	.0220521	.0138613	.0109549
3.95	.0155159	.0382150	.3930687	.0402002	.0233969	.0143805	.0112766
4.00	.0149260	.0348273	....	.0447780	.0248767	.0149260	.0116091
4.05	.0143920	.0320549	.4029757	.0503720	.0265116	.0154991	.0119525
4.10	.0139065	.0297444	.2039616	.0573642	.0283280	.0161022	.0123080
4.15	.0134631	.0277893	.1376231	.0663540	.0303580	.0167379	.0126758
4.20	.0130567	.0261134	.1044536	.0783402	.0326418	.0174089	.0130567
4.25	.0126830	.0246613	.0845532	.0951223	.0352305	.0181185	.0134516
4.30	.0123379	.0233906	.0712855	.1202944	.0381887	.0188696	.0138611
4.35	.0120183	.0222693	.0618086	.1622475	.0416019	.0196664	.0142859
4.40	.0117216	.0212726	.0547008	.2461535	.0455840	.0205128	.0147271
4.45	.0114453	.0203807	.0491724	.4978708	.0502900	.0214138	.0151856
4.50	.0111874	.0195780	.0447497	....	.0559371	.0223748	.0156624
4.55	.0109462	.0188517	.0411310	.5089964	.0628391	.0234021	.0161586
4.60	.0107200	.0181914	.0381154	.2572791	.0714664	.0245028	.0166755
4.65	.0105075	.0175886	.0355637	.1733731	.0825586	.0256849	.0172143
4.70	.0103075	.0170359	.0333765	.1314200	.0973481	.0269579	.0177766
4.75	.0101188	.0165274	.0314808	.1062679	.1180532	.0283328	.0183638
4.80	.0099407	.0160581	.0298221	.0894664	.1491106	.0298221	.0189777
4.85	.0097722	.0156257	.0283585	.0774795	.2008728	.0314410	.0196201
4.90	.0096125	.0152198	.0270575	.0684893	.3043969	.0332069	.0202931
4.95	.0094610	.0148441	.0258934	.0614968	.6149681	.0351410	.0209989
5.00	.0093171	.0144933	.0248457	.0559028	....	.0372685	.0217400

APPENDIX III.

Summary of Compound Interest Processes.

To find the Ratio of Increase

    Add 1 to the Rate of Interest.

To find the Amount *of* $1

    Multiply 1 by the Ratio as many times as there are periods.

To find the Present Worth *of* $1, *or to* discount $1

    Divide 1 by the Ratio as many times as there are periods.

To find the Total Interest

    Subtract 1 from the Amount.

To find the Total Discount

    Subtract the Present Worth from 1.

To find the Amount *of an* Annuity *of* $1

    Divide the Total Interest by the Rate of Interest.

To find the Present Worth *of an* Annuity *of* $1

    Divide the Total Discount by the Rate of Interest.

To find the Rent *of an* Annuity *worth* $1, *or what Annuity can be bought for* $1

    Divide 1 by the Present Worth of the Annuity.

To find what Annuity (Sinking Fund) *will produce* $1

    Divide 1 by the Amount of the Annuity.

To find the Premium *or* Discount *on a* Bond

    Consider the Difference of Interest as an Annuity to be valued, and find its Present Worth.

List of Titles

Accounting History and the Development of a Profession

Management Accounting Research: A Review and Annotated Bibliography.
Charles F. Klemstine and Michael W. Maher. New York, 1984.

Accounting Literature in Non-Accounting Journals: An Annotated Bibliography.
Panadda Tantral. New York, 1984.

The Evolution of Behavioral Accounting Research: An Overview.
Robert H. Ashton, editor. New York, 1984.

Some Early Contributions to the Study of Audit Judgment.
Robert H. Ashton, editor. New York, 1984.

Depreciation and Capital Maintenance.
Richard P. Brief, editor. New York, 1984.

The Case for Continuously Contemporary Accounting.
G. W. Dean and M. C. Wells, editors. New York, 1984.

Studies of Company Records: 1830–1974.
J. R. Edwards, editor. New York, 1984.

European Equity Markets: Risk, Return, and Efficiency.
Gabriel Hawawini and Pierre Michel, editors. New York, 1984.

Transactions of the Chartered Accountants Students' Societies of Edinburgh and Glasgow: A Selection of Writings, 1886–1958.
Thomas A. Lee, editor. New York, 1984.

The Development of Double Entry: Selected Essays.
Christopher Nobes, editor. New York, 1984.

Papers on Accounting History.
R. H. Parker. New York, 1984.

Collected Papers on Accounting and Accounting Education.
David Solomons. New York, 1984.

The General Principles of the Science of Accounts and the Accountancy of Investment.
Charles E. Sprague. New York, 1984.

Selected Papers on Accounting, Auditing, and Professional Problems.
Edward Stamp. New York, 1984.

Factory Accounts.
John Whitmore. New York, 1984.

Sourcebook on Accounting Principles and Auditing Procedures: 1917–1953 (in two volumes).
Stephen A. Zeff and Maurice Moonitz, editors. New York, 1984.

The First Fifty Years 1913–1963.
Arthur Andersen Company. Chicago, 1963.

Paciolo on Accounting.
R. Gene Brown and Kenneth S. Johnston. New York, 1963.

The Early History of Coopers & Lybrand.
Coopers & Lybrand. New York, 1984.

Report of the Trial . . . Against the Directors and the Manager of the City of Glasgow Bank.
Charles Tennant Couper. Edinburgh, 1879.

Development of Accounting Thought.
Harvey T. Deinzer. New York, 1965.

The Principles of Auditing.
F.R.M. De Paula. London, 1915.

The Accountant, or, the Method of Bookkeeping Deduced from Clear Principles, and Illustrated by a Variety of Examples.
James Dodson. London, 1750.

A Common Sense Method of Double Entry Bookkeeping, on First Principles, as Suggested by De Morgan. Part I, Theoretical.
S. Dyer. London, 1897.

Economics of Fatigue and Unrest and the Efficiency of Labour in English and American Industry.
P. Sargant Florence. London, 1923.

Haskins & Sells: Our First Seventy-Five Years.
Arthur B. Foye. New York, 1970.

The History of the Society of Incorporated Accountants, 1885–1957.
A. A. Garrett. Oxford, 1961.

The Game of Budget Control.
Geert Hofstede. Assen, 1967.

The History of The Institute of Chartered Accountants in England and Wales 1880–1965, and of Its Founder Accountancy Bodies 1870–1880.
Sir Harold Howitt. London, 1966.

History of the Chartered Accountants of Scotland from the Earliest Times to 1954.
Institute of Chartered Accountants of Scotland. Edinburgh, 1954.

Accounting Thought and Education: Six English Pioneers.
J. Kitchen and R. H. Parker. London, 1980.

The Evolution of Corporate Financial Reporting.
T. A. Lee and R. H. Parker. Middlesex, 1979.

Accounting in Scotland: A Historical Bibliography.
Janet E. Pryce-Jones and R. H. Parker. Edinburgh, 1976.

A History of Accountants in Ireland.
H. W. Robinson. Dublin, 1964.

The Sixth International Congress on Accounting.
London, 1952.

The Accomptant's Oracle: or, Key to Science, Being a Compleat Practical System of Book-keeping.
Wardbaugh Thompson. York, 1777.

Accountancy in Transition

The Tangled Web of Price Variation Accounting: The Development of Ideas Underlying Professional Prescriptions in Six Countries.
F. L. Clarke. New York, 1982.

Beta Alpha Psi, From Alpha to Omega: Pursuing a Vision of Professional Education for Accountants, 1919–1945.
Terry K. Sheldahl. New York, 1982.

Four Classics on the Theory of Double-Entry Bookkeeping.
Richard P. Brief, editor. New York, 1982.

Forerunners of Realizable Values Accounting in Financial Reporting.
G. W. Dean and M. C. Wells, editors. New York, 1982.

Accounting Queries.
Harold C. Edey. New York, 1982.

The Development of Accounting Theory: Significant Contributors to Accounting Thought in the 20th Century.
Michael Gaffikin and Michael Aitken, editors. New York, 1982.

Studies in Social and Private Accounting.
Solomon Fabricant. New York, 1982.

Bond Duration and Immunization: Early Developments and Recent Contributions.
Gabriel A. Hawawini, editor. New York, 1982.

Further Essays on the History of Accounting.
Basil S. Yamey. New York, 1982.

Accounting Principles Through The Years: The Views of Professional and Academic Leaders 1938–1954.
Stephen A. Zeff, editor. New York, 1982.

The Accounting Postulates and Principles Controversy of the 1960s.
Stephen A. Zeff, editor. New York, 1982.

Fiftieth Anniversary Celebration.
American Institute of Accountants. New York, 1937.

Library Catalogue.
American Institute of Accountants. New York, 1919.

Four Essays in Accounting Theory.
F. Sewell Bray. London, 1953. *bound with*
Some Accounting Terms and Concepts.
Institute of Chartered Accountants in England and Wales and The National Institute of Economic and Social Research. Cambridge, 1951.

Accounting in Disarray.
R. J. Chambers. Melbourne, 1973.

The Balance-Sheet.
Charles B. Couchman. New York, 1924.

Audits.
Arthur E. Cutforth. London, 1906.

Methods of Amalgamation.
Arthur E. Cutforth. London, 1926.

Deloitte & Co. 1845–1956.
Sir Russell Kettle. Oxford, 1958. *bound with*
Fifty-seven Years in an Accountant's Office.
Ernest Cooper. London, 1921.

Accountants and the Law of Negligence.
R. W. Dickerson. Toronto, 1966.

Consolidated Statements.
H. A. Finney. New York, 1922.

The Rate of Interest.
Irving Fisher. New York, 1907.

Holding Companies and Their Published Accounts.
Sir Gilbert Garnsey. London, 1923. *bound with*
Limitations of a Balance Sheet.
Sir Gilbert Garnsey. London, 1928.

Accounting Concepts of Profit.
Stephen Gilman. New York, 1939.

**An Introduction to Merchandise, Parts IV and V
(Italian Bookkeeping and Practical Bookkeeping).**
Robert Hamilton. Edinburgh, 1788.

The Merchant's Magazine: or, Trades-man's Treasury.
Edward Hatton. London, 1695.

The Law of Accounting and Financial Statements.
George S. Hills. Boston, 1957.

International Congress on Accounting 1929.
New York, 1930.

Fourth International Congress on Accounting 1933.
London, 1933.

Magnificent Masquerade.
Charles Keats. New York, 1964.

Profit Measurement and Price Changes.
Kenneth Lacey. London, 1952.

The American Accomptant.
Chauncey Lee. Lansingburgh, 1797.

Consolidated Balance Sheets.
George Hills Newlove. New York, 1926.

Consolidated and Other Group Accounts.
T. B. Robson. London, 1950.

Accounting Method.
C. Rufus Rorem. Chicago, 1928.

Shareholder's Money.
Horace B. Samuel. London, 1933.

Standardized Accountancy in Germany. (With a new appendix.)
H. W. Singer. Cambridge, 1943.

**The Securities and Exchange Commission in the Matter of McKesson
& Robbins, Inc. Report on Investigation.**
Washington, D. C., 1940.

**The Securities and Exchange Commission in the Matter of McKesson
& Robbins, Inc. Testimony of Expert Witnesses.**
Washington, D. C., 1939.

Accounting in England and Scotland: 1543–1800.
B. S. Yamey, H. C. Edey, Hugh W. Thomson. London, 1963.

DATE DUE

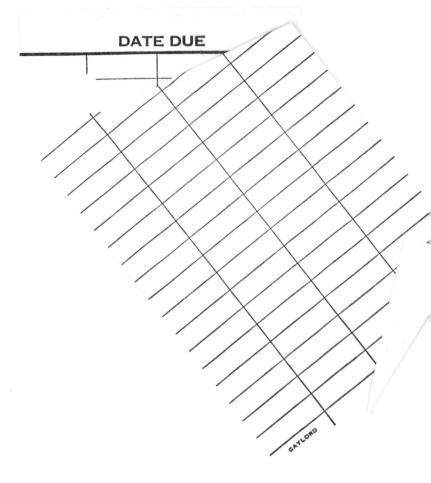

GAYLORD